Reader's Digest
Home Survey
Manual

Reader's Digest
Home Survey
Manual

What to look for when buying or selling your home

Published by
The Reader's Digest Association Limited
London • New York • Sydney • Montreal

Contents

Energy efficiency

About this book

If you are buying or selling a home this book shows you how to spot potential problems with a property at the beginning of the process, saving time and renegotiation as completion date approaches. Even if you are not moving house, this book will help you to avoid costly emergency repairs by identifying defects in their early stages.

You have an annual service and MOT on your car; you may even have an annual health check yourself; so why not treat your home the same, and take time to assess its condition, inside and out, once a year? A simple and methodical annual survey will enable you to spot small defects in and around your home before they turn into large ones.

Nipping problems in the bud will save you time and money in the long run. Small faults are generally easier to fix than major ones and will not have had a chance to allow other, secondary damage to occur. A small split in the felt covering of a flat roof, for example, is a simple DIY fix, but if left undetected water will seep through the roof, rotting the timbers and penetrating as damp into the ceiling or internal walls of the rooms below. By the time the problem is clearly visible on the inside, you will have several more complex jobs to tackle on top of the original small one.

When you are selling your home

If you are thinking of selling your house, it is even more important that your property should be in good condition before you put it on the market. Not only will this help to ensure that you get the best possible price for your house, it can also mean the difference between completing and losing a sale by minimising the chances of the homebuyer's survey uncovering any nasty surprises.

You may decide to include a voluntary Home Condition Report in your Home Information Pack (see page 9) and this will make potential buyers aware of any work that needs to be done before they make an offer. But whether the survey is done before you put your house on the market or after you have found a purchaser, even small faults that come to light can lead to lengthy haggling over the price that can hold up the sale.

Doing your own preliminary survey gives you the chance to fix problems you discover before you start the process of selling. This book's clear advice explains exactly what is involved in each repair or replacement job so that you can weigh up whether it is worth doing the remedial work yourself or whether to prepare yourself to negotiate with buyers over the costs they have ahead of them.

When you are buying a home

There is a lot to consider when viewing a property that you are interested in purchasing and it is all too easy to be distracted by decor, the surroundings and even the person showing you around. Armed with this book and its expert tips and advice, you will know exactly what to look out for as you tour a property, understand how to spot problems or potential problems, and assess what is likely to be involved in putting them right.

A high proportion of sales fall through when purchasers receive their surveyor's report and discover that there are jobs that need to be done that may be both costly and disruptive. Going into a purchase with the knowledge obtained with the help of this book means that you can evaluate right at the beginning, before you even instruct your surveyor to visit the property, whether you are prepared to take on the projects involved and you will also feel confident that you can make a fair offer for the property.

How to use this book

Work through the book, assessing each individual part of your home, from the front door to the loft and boundary fences. For each section – windows, floors, taps and more – you will find a clear explanation of the different construction types you might find (depending on the age and style of your house), expert pointers on the most common problems and how to identify them, and then illustrated step-by-step instructions for all the jobs you are likely to have to tackle, from patching damaged plaster or chipped skirting boards to replacing a rotten section of a wooden window sill or a dangerous broken floorboard.

Chapter One takes you round the exterior of the property, examining the walls, roof, gutters and drains, paths and driveway, and the garden walls and fences. You'll also find advice on how to assess the services to the property and whether they may need updating, although full electrical and plumbing surveys are jobs that should always be left to the professionals.

Chapter Two turns to the interior, inspecting and fixing problems with the walls, floors, ceilings, stairs, internal doors and the accessible plumbing in kitchens and bathrooms, such as taps and drainage traps.

Chapter Three helps you to assess the energy efficiency of your home and shows you how you can improve it with better loft insulation, smarter central heating controls and effective draught-proofing measures on all your doors and windows. Doing all you can to maximise your home's efficiency in its consumption of energy for heating and lighting will save you money in energy bills – and go towards saving the planet at the same time. But it will also reap dividends when you come to sell your home, by attracting buyers with a good energy rating in your Home Information Pack. You can find more information about this and what an energy efficiency assessment entails on pages 110–111.

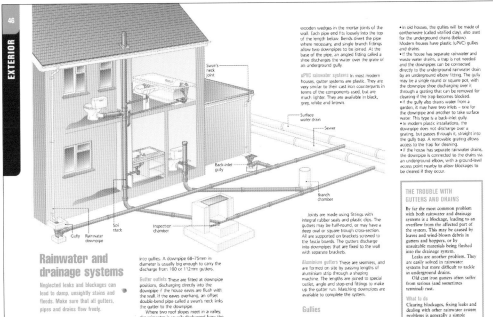

46 EXTERIOR

47 DRAINAGE

wooden wedges in the mortar joints of the wall. Each pipe end fits loosely into the top of the length below. Bends divert the pipe where necessary, and single branch fittings allow two downpipes to be joined. At the base of the pipe, an angled fitting called a shoe discharges the water over the grate of an underground gully.

uPVC rainwater systems In most modern houses, gutter systems are plastic. They are very similar to their cast iron counterparts in terms of the components used, but are much lighter. They are available in black, grey, white and brown.

Joints are made using fittings with integral rubber seals and plastic clips. The gutters may be half-round, or may have a deep oval or square trough cross-section. All are supported on brackets screwed to the fascia boards. The gutters discharge into downpipes that are fixed to the wall with separate brackets.

Aluminium gutters These are seamless, and are formed on site by passing lengths of aluminium strip through a shaping machine. The lengths are joined to special outlets, angle and stop-end fittings to make up the gutter run. Matching downpipes are available to complete the system.

Gullies

At ground level, downpipes discharge into an underground fitting called a gully. If rainwater and waste water flow into the same drains, the gully contains a U-bend which prevents drain smells from rising up the downpipes. The bend also acts as a trap for debris washed down from the roof slope, preventing it from being washed into the drains.

• In old houses, the gullies will be made of earthenware (called vitrified clay), also used for the underground drains (below). Modern houses have plastic (uPVC) gullies and drains.
• If the house has separate rainwater and waste water drains, a trap is not needed and the downpipes can be connected directly to the underground rainwater drain by an underground elbow fitting. The gully may be a single round or square pot, with the downpipe shoe discharging over it through a grating that can be removed for cleaning if the trap becomes blocked.
• If the gully also drains water from a garden, it may have two inlets – one for the downpipe and another to take surface water. This type is a back-inlet gully.
• In modern plastic installations, the downpipe does not discharge over a grating, but passes through it, straight into the gully trap. A removable grating allows access to the trap for cleaning.
• If the house has separate rainwater drains, the downpipe is connected to the drains via an underground elbow, with a ground-level access point nearby to allow blockages to be cleared if they occur.

Labels on diagram: Swan's neck joint · Surface water drain · Sewer · Back-inlet gully · Branch chamber · Soil stack · Inspection chamber · Gully · Rainwater downpipe

Rainwater and drainage systems

Neglected leaks and blockages can lead to damp, unsightly stains and floods. Make sure that all gutters, pipes and drains flow freely.

Water running off a roof is collected in gutters fixed to the fascia boards. The gutters must be big enough to collect the occasional downpour without overflowing, and for most houses a gutter 100 or 112mm in width will do the job.

They discharge the water they collect into downpipes, which run down the house walls to ground level and empty the water into gullies. A downpipe 68–75mm in diameter is usually big enough to carry the discharge from 100 or 112mm gutters.

Gutter outlets These are fitted at downpipe positions, discharging directly into the downpipe if the house eaves are flush with the wall. If the eaves overhang, an offset double-bend pipe called a swan's neck links the gutter to the downpipe.

Where two roof slopes meet in a valley, the rainwater is usually discharged from the valley gutter into a fitting called a hopper. A downpipe runs from the hopper down to ground level. A rainwater hopper may also collect waste water from upstairs baths and washbasins.

Cast iron downpipes Iron pipes have integral fixing lugs that are secured to the house walls with large pipe nails driven into

THE TROUBLE WITH GUTTERS AND DRAINS

By far the most common problem with both rainwater and drainage systems is a blockage, leading to an overflow from the affected part of the system. This may be caused by leaves and wind-blown debris in gutters and hoppers, or by unsuitable materials being flushed into the drainage system.

Leaks are another problem. They are easily solved in rainwater systems but more difficult to tackle in underground drains. Old cast iron gutters often suffer from serious (and sometimes terminal) rust.

What to do
Clearing blockages, fixing leaks and dealing with other rainwater system problems is generally a simple matter of routine maintenance (see pages 49–55). You can tackle most drain blockages yourself with the aid of a set of drain rods, which you can buy or hire when required (see pages 53–55).

Home Information Packs

From 1 June 2007, all home owners in England and Wales will be required to prepare a Home Information Pack for potential buyers before putting their home up for sale.

Providing information on searches, guarantees of work, building control certificates and leases up front aims to reduce some of the stress and uncertainty out of negotiating for and buying a home.

The packs give potential buyers full access to information previously obtained during the conveyancing process, only after an offer has been made and accepted and solicitors instructed. When problems and queries were brought to light during conveyancing it could create hold-ups that would affect a long chain of other sales and purchases, may lead to an anxious renegotiation of price or even cause the sale to fall through. Under the new system, only a homebuyer's survey still needs to be undertaken – usually for the purpose of a mortgage offer.

Do I need to produce a pack for my property?

Most residential property sales require a Home Information Pack to be presented to potential purchasers. Exceptions are:
Non-residential properties: commercial properties, such as shops.
Mixed residential and commercial properties. This may be a shop with flats above that is being sold as a single unit.
Tenanted properties, where the property is being sold with a sitting tenant.
Short leases: properties with a lease of less than 21 years.

Can I produce the pack myself?

It is possible for a vendor to carry out his own conveyancing when selling a home, and there is no legal reason not to compile your own Home Information Pack.

THE 'SELL BY' DATE

Home Information Packs are valid for as long as a home is being continuously marketed, while allowing for a break while a vendor changes agents or while a sale that subsequently falls through is being negotiated. The packs do not have an expiry time and do not need to be revised during a lengthy period on the market, but it is generally advised that searches should be repeated at six monthly intervals.

However, doing the work yourself may lead to problems later in the process. Mortgage lenders for your purchaser will almost certainly insist on a professional conveyancer; other parties in the sale or elsewhere in the chain are often uncomfortable at the thought of a DIY job and may pull out of the deal rather than risk something going wrong in the last stages of the purchase; and the risk of problems that could result in costly and time-consuming legal disputes is far higher than when using a professional.

The home condition report

In the initial plans for the Home Information Packs, a detailed home condition report, similar to the survey carried out by most home buyers, was to be included. This is no longer a requirement, but sellers can still 'top up' their packs to include a voluntary report, based on a professional survey of the property.

These will cover the aspects of the house and grounds included in this book, and conducting your own preliminary survey and remedying any problems you uncover can help to ensure a favourable report to include in your seller's pack. While it is voluntary to include a condition report, it is hoped that they will be accepted by buyers and mortgage lenders, and will eliminate the need for a purchaser to instruct their own surveyor. This should speed up the sales process and result in fewer failed transactions, where surveys uncover problems that lead to renegotiations on price and terms of sale.

What do the packs include?

 Terms of sale Full descriptive details of the property for sale, usually drawn up by the vendor's estate agent.

 Evidence of title Land Registry details or copies of the deeds to the property, confirming ownership.

 Searches Replies to standard searches, such as planning permissions, water and drainage and road schemes planned for the surrounding area.

 Consents and approvals for any planning requests, listed building works and works subject to Building Regulations control on the property.

 Guarantees Certificates and any active warranties for any building or remedial work carried out on the property, plus any valid new homes (NHBC) warranty on a recently built property.

 Forms detailing household fixtures and fittings included in or excluded from the sale.

 Forms detailing any other appropriate information about the property.

 An energy efficiency report on the property, together with recommendations of improvements that could be made (see pages 110–111).

 Where the construction of a property is not yet completed, a report will be included in the pack.

Home Information Packs for leasehold properties with leases longer than 21 years should also include:

 The lease.

✔ **Details of the landlord** or managing agent.

✔ **Any regulations** stipulated by the landlord or managing agent.

✔ **Full details of any regular service charges** applicable to the property and receipts or any recent requests for ground rent and insurance payments.

✔ **Details of any current and planned works** relating to the property.

Certificate of Treatment
by
London & Home Counties
TIMBER PRESERVATION

This is to Certify that

Address and Location of Property   Ground Floor: Kitchen/Diner

Exact Description of Area Treated

As per Survey Report & Specification dated   23 September 1999 – T5167
has been properly treated in accordance with the schedule submitted, using high
grade materials, against   rising damp (injection of new DPC
only).

and is guaranteed against further attack from this type of
RISING DAMPNESS /
(subject to the provisions detailed on the back of this document) for a period of
30 YEARS   from   11 October 1999.

Signed on behalf of the Company by

p.p. LONDON & HOME COUNTIES TIMBER PRESERVATION

THIS CERTIFICATE IS TRANSFERABLE.

Exterior & services

Foundations

Firm foundations are vitally important. Spotting problems here can save you from a purchase in need of costly and complicated repair.

It was not until 1879 that the law required houses to be built with a concrete strip foundation. It had to be just 230mm thick. Older properties may have little more than rammed earth or stone foundations, with stepped brickwork built up to ground level to help to spread the load of the walls. By contrast, modern homes often have deep concrete trench foundations. The area within modern concrete foundations is usually covered with a reinforced concrete ground slab; older properties usually had suspended timber ground floors.

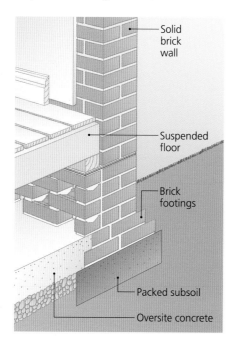

Solid brick wall

Suspended floor

Brick footings

Packed subsoil

Oversite concrete

What to do when cracks appear

If you start to notice cracks developing in walls, or around the edges of solid floor slabs, seek professional help without delay. The best place to start is the building control department of your local authority. The inspectors will be familiar with local soil conditions and they will also be able to put you in contact with approved contractors if remedial work is necessary.

THE TROUBLE WITH FOUNDATIONS

Foundations can suffer from several problems, all producing similar symptoms: small cracks in the house walls to begin with, then larger ones – often linking door and window openings, and following a zig-zag path up the walls as mortar joints fail. Here are some common problems affecting foundations.

Settlement All new houses settle to some degree as the ground is compacted by the new load imposed on it. The result is usually a few small cracks, which stop developing when settlement is complete, and which can be repaired with no risk of recurrence.

Differential settlement An extension or addition to a property may be built with different foundations from the original, and the new part may settle and start to separate from the existing building over time. The problem was common with bay windows and back additions in Victorian houses, and is seen today with home extensions.

Ground movement The moisture content of the ground beneath the house changes with the seasons. This is pronounced with clay soils, particularly during a severe drought. Frost heave, caused by water within the soil freezing and expanding upwards, may also displace the foundations; it occurs mainly in porous sandy and chalk subsoils. Ground movement can be caused by trees too close to the house, either sucking moisture from the ground as they grow, or no longer doing so if they are felled.

Overloading Foundations may be overloaded after structural alterations. For example, removing a load-bearing internal wall and installing a rolled steel joist (RSJ).

Subsidence True subsidence is due to the collapse of underground chambers such as caves or disused mine shafts. The effects on a building can be catastrophic.

Exterior walls

Walls vary in construction and finish, which may be purely decorative or have weather-proofing properties. Minor problems are easy to repair, but look out for more serious faults.

Solid walls Houses built before about 1920 have solid walls of brick or stone – brick walls are usually about 230mm thick; the thickness of stone walls depends on the type of stone used. Buildings taller than two storeys, such as Georgian terraced houses, often have thicker walls in the lower storeys to carry the extra load.

Cavity walls Houses built since about 1920 have cavity walls – developed as a way to prevent damp from penetrating. Early examples have two brick walls (called leaves) about 100mm thick separated by an open cavity 50–75mm wide. The two leaves were held together by metal wall ties.
Blockwork Newer houses have the inner leaf of the cavity wall (and the outer one too if the exterior is rendered or has tiling or weather-boarding) built of insulating blockwork rather than brick. This reduces heat losses through the walls, and their thermal efficiency can be increased still further by using insulation in the wall cavities. This may fill the cavity completely, or may be held against the inner leaf so that water penetrating the outer leaf can run down to ground level rather than across to the inner leaf. The two leaves of the wall are tied together with galvanised wire, stainless steel or plastic wall ties.
Timber-framed walls An increasing number of new houses are built with timber-framed exterior walls. The inner leaf, of prefabricated timber-framed panels, carries the load of the upper storeys and the roof. The decorative outer leaf, of brick-work or weather-proofed blockwork, is tied to the inner leaf by wall ties, with a cavity between the two. Insulation is incorporated within the wall panels, so the cavity is kept clear. The panels also have a plastic vapour barrier on the inside to stop moisture from the house condensing within the insulation and causing the timber frame to rot.

Wall finishes

External finishes The walls may be exposed brick or stone with mortar pointing. Solid brick walls will show headers (the ends of

THE TROUBLE WITH WALLS

Water and frost are the biggest enemies of exterior walls. Defective pointing (page 14), damaged rendering (pages 14–15) and failed weatherproofing (page 16) can allow moisture to penetrate the structure, causing damp patches to appear indoors. Damp masonry can be damaged by frost, which freezes water within the wall structure and makes it expand, splitting the faces off bricks and detaching rendering from the masonry.

Settlement of the foundations (see opposite) can cause severe cracking in external walls. Failure of the wall ties can cause a cavity wall to bow outwards.

What to do
Most minor faults can be repaired by a competent do-it-yourselfer; the cross-references above will take you to the relevant pages of the book.

the bricks) alternating with stretchers (their long sides) laid in one of several regular patterns called bonds. Cavity brick walls will show only stretchers, laid with a half-brick overlap in what is known as stretcher bond.
Rendering Cement or lime mortar applied as a weatherproof coating may be smooth or textured, and there are many regional variations. A universal rendered finish is pebble-dashing, created by bedding small stones in the mortar coat. Rendering and pebble-dashing are often painted to improve their looks and weather resistance.

Other external wall finishes include clay tiles hung on timber battens, timber weather-boarding, timber shingles and plastic cladding. Timber finishes may be left to weather, or may be stained or painted for decorative effect.

Internal finishes Masonry walls are usually given an internal finish of plaster – one or two undercoats and a thin finish coat. Lime plasters are found in older houses, whereas modern houses have gypsum-based plaster which is thinner and harder. Some older houses have plaster applied over wooden laths fixed to wall battens. A similar effect is achieved in modern houses by dry-lining walls with plasterboard on wall battens, as an alternative to wet plaster. Timber-framed houses have plasterboard cladding on the inner face of the wall panels.

Minor repairs to walls

Cracks, deteriorating mortar, damp and damaged brickwork are all easily repaired when the problem is small.

Repointing a wall

Where mortar joints in a wall are cracked or crumbling, use a raking out tool or a club hammer and plugging chisel to take out the old mortar to a depth of about 15mm, ready for repointing.

Before you start One problem when you are patching a number of joints is to match the colour of the mortar with that of the surrounding joints. The only way to do this is to experiment with a few different mortar mixes, using varying amounts of sand and lime. Take a note of each mix and repoint a few joints at a time. Wait a week or two for the mortar to dry thoroughly and show its final colour before you decide on the best mix to complete the job.

Before you apply new mortar, clean any dust from the joints then brush water into them. If you do not wet them, the joints will soak up moisture from the mortar and it will dry out too fast. As you repoint the joint, take care to match the shape of the finish with the surrounding joints.

Dealing with a crack

Mortar is meant to be weaker than bricks or masonry so that it offers less resistance if movement beneath the foundations causes any strain on the wall. The mortar will crack before the bricks or masonry.

A single crack confined to a mortar joint, even through several courses, usually indicates slight soil settlement. A repair can be made by repointing.

A single brick cracked by minor settlement can be replaced by yourself (below). If a crack runs through more than the odd brick, there is a more serious strain on the foundations. Get a professional builder to deal with it as soon as possible.

Replacing a damaged brick

Remove a damaged brick by chipping away the surrounding mortar with a club hammer and cold chisel.

You can speed up the process by drilling a series of holes into the mortar first. Drill to a depth of about 100mm, then cut into the mortar all round to release the damaged brick. Chop as much mortar out of the resulting cavity as you can, ready for the new brick to be fitted. Dampen the cavity very well. Spread mortar on the base of the cavity and on the top and sides of the new brick. Tap the brick into the cavity with the trowel handle. When it is properly seated, trim away the excess mortar. Point the joints to match the others on the wall.

Repairing cracks on a rendered wall

Before you start Hairline crazing on the surface of rendering does not need filling. Cracks that go deeper should be filled to keep the wall weatherproof. Fill the cracks with exterior filler or with rendering. Filler is convenient but uneconomical for more than one or two cracks. You can buy dry-mixed rendering or make your own. The repair will show until the wall is repainted; an invisible repair is impossible to achieve.

Tools *Filling knife; brush; wet sponge or cloth; old paintbrush. Perhaps a bolster chisel and club hammer and a ladder.*

Materials *PVA adhesive; rendering or exterior filler.*

1 Draw the edge of a filling knife through the crack to form it into a V with the point of the V at the surface of the rendering and the wider part against the wall.
  You can use a bolster chisel and club hammer instead of the filling knife if you find it easier. The shape will anchor the filler below the surface and the crack is unlikely to open again.

2 Brush out the fragments and dust from the cavity to leave it as clean as possible.

3 Wet the cavity with a sponge or cloth dipped in water.

4 Paint all the inside of the cavity with PVA adhesive to improve adhesion of the filler.

5 Press the filler or rendering into the crack with the filling knife. Prod the knife into the cavity to make sure there are no air pockets in it. Smooth the filling level with the wall surface. Redecorate the wall when the filler has dried.

Patching large holes

Before you start When large slabs of rendering fall away from the wall, it is usually because a weak rendering mix has been used and become porous, or because damp has penetrated behind the layer of rendering, perhaps through a crack.
  Sometimes the rendering may appear intact, when in fact it has separated from the wall behind. Check the rendering from time to time, tapping it lightly with a hammer; undamaged areas will make a dead sound while defective areas give a hollow sound or fall away.
  Carry out rendering work in mild weather. Frost can freeze the water in the rendering, which may cause premature cracking.

Tools *Bolster chisel; club hammer; brush; wet sponge or cloth; steel plastering trowel; old pointed trowel or square of wood with nails driven through to project at about 38mm intervals; straight edged length of wood longer than the width of the patch; damp sponge or clean wooden float. Perhaps a ladder and a plugging chisel.*

Materials *Rendering.*

1 Use the bolster chisel and hammer to cut away any loose rendering to leave a sound edge round the patch.

2 Clean out any crumbling joints in the brickwork or masonry. Clean them out to a depth of 15mm with the plugging chisel and club hammer. Brush out all debris.

3 Thoroughly wet the area to be repaired with a sponge or cloth soaked in water. This prevents rendering from losing moisture into the wall and drying too quickly, which could cause crumbling later.

4 Apply the first coat of rendering. Take some of the mixture on the steel trowel with the handle downwards. Spread it onto the wall, starting from the bottom of the patch and pressing the lower edge of the trowel hard against the wall as you sweep it smoothly upwards. Continue until the rendering is smooth and about 5mm below the level of the wall surface.

5 As the rendering begins to stiffen after about 20 minutes – scratch a criss-cross of lines in it with the old trowel or spiked wood to make a key for the top coat.

6 Leave the first coat to dry for at least 14 hours, then apply the finishing coat. Use the same rendering mixture as for the floating coat. This time, start at the top left of the patch. Sweep the trowel lightly across from left to right to spread the rendering over the area, leaving it standing slightly proud of the surface.

7 Continue applying trowel loads from top to bottom down the patch spreading them from left to right. Mix more small batches of rendering as necessary, but work quickly.

8 Just before the rendering begins to set – about 15 minutes after it has been applied – draw the straight-edged piece of wood upwards over the rendering to level it with the wall. Hold the wood horizontally and make sure that you are pressing its ends firmly against the wall on either side of the patch. If any hollows are showing after levelling off, fill them quickly with more rendering and level them with the straight-edged piece of wood. As the rendering starts to set, smooth its surface gently with a damp sponge or a damp wooden float.

Repairing pebbledash

It is simple enough to repair damaged pebbledash, but the repair will be visible unless the wall is to be painted because the new chippings and the rendering beneath will not match the original colour. You will need about 5kg of chippings to cover a square metre.

Tools *Cold chisel; club hammer; brush; wet sponge or cloth; steel trowel; sheet of polythene; small scoop; wooden float. Perhaps a ladder.*

Materials *Soft sand and cement or dry ready-mix rendering mortar; PVA building adhesive; water; chippings.*

1 Prepare the area for repair as for Patching large holes (page 15) and mix and lay on a first coat of rendering in the same way, but leave it about 15mm below the level of the wall surface.

2 Wash the chippings and drain them in a garden sieve.

3 Mix the rendering for the top coat, known as the butter coat. Use five parts of sand to one cement and add some PVA building adhesive.
Mix it to a slightly softer consistency than the first coat to make sure that it is still soft when you apply the chippings.
Apply the top coat; if you have a large area to repair, work on a section which you can complete within 20 minutes before the coat starts to set.

4 Spread a sheet of polythene on the ground below the repair. Throw small scoops of pebbles hard at the rendering until it is evenly covered. Gather up and re-use the chippings that fall to the ground.

Alternatively Lift batches of pebbles up to the wall on a hawk and use a float to push them off the hawk and into the wet mortar.

5 When you have pebbledashed the patched area, press the wooden float lightly all over it to bed the chippings into the surface. Continue in the same way until the repair is complete.

PROTECTING CLADDING

Timber cladding, which forms part of an exterior wall, must be protected by preservative or paint if it is not to be affected by damp, otherwise wet rot may set in. Plastic cladding is not affected by damp but gaps surrounding the cladding must be tightly sealed. Follow the same procedure as for sealing gaps round window frames (page 23).

Keeping out damp with silicone water repellent

Silicone water repellent will normally cure damp problems on external walls. It stops rain from getting into the brick but it lets the wall 'breathe' so that moisture already in the material can evaporate.

If damp patches persist, you should seek professional advice.

Tools *Bucket of water; wire brush; a clean old paintbrush, 100–150mm wide; paint kettle. Perhaps a ladder.*

Materials *Silicone water repellent such as Aquaseal 66; white spirit for cleaning brush.*

1 Clean the surface with water and the wire brush. Wait until the surface has dried.

2 Tape paper over the window glass, frame and ledges. You will not be able to remove splashes of silicone from them. Cover any part of a drive or path adjoining the wall you are treating. The silicone could otherwise cause blotches.

3 Pour the repellent into a paint kettle and apply a generous amount of the liquid with an old paintbrush, so that you can see it flowing down the wall.

4 If the surface soaks up all the liquid – because it is very porous – apply a second coat before the first coat dries.

5 Use white spirit to clean the paintbrush and the paint kettle when the job is finished.

Dealing with efflorescence

The white powdery deposit called efflorescence is caused by dampness, which draws chemical salts from the bricks or mortar to the surface. It is harmless, and will disappear from a newly built wall once it has dried out.

You can discourage efflorescence by coating a wall with a silicone-based water repellent. If efflorescence does form, brush it off or treat it with a chemical masonry cleaner. Do not wash off efflorescence; the damp aggravates the problem.

Recognising rising damp

Damp patches at skirting-board level on an interior wall, or a tidemark as high as a metre above floor level, are two signs of damp rising from the ground.

Damp prevention

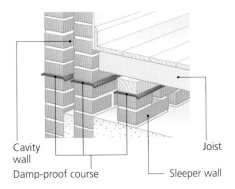

Cavity wall

Joist

Damp-proof course

Sleeper wall

To prevent damp from rising, houses are built with a damp-proof course (DPC). This is an impermeable plastic strip in modern houses, or a layer of slates or hard engineering bricks in older properties.

In most houses (except very old ones built without a DPC), you will see a thicker than usual horizontal line of pointing about 150mm above ground level, running right round the external walls. This line indicates the position of the DPC.

Defects in the damp-proofing

If the DPC deteriorates or becomes damaged, or if there is no DPC, damp is able to rise through the house walls. Rising damp will also occur if the DPC is bridged by damp material reaching above it against the outside wall – a rockery, for example, a flowerbed or even a temporary pile of building sand.

Rising damp may occur because a path or drive is too close to, or is higher than, the level of the DPC. Paths and drives must be at least 150mm below the DPC so that rainwater cannot splash above it. Where necessary, lower the path or drive surface if at all possible.

Alternatively, dig a 300mm wide channel alongside the outside wall of the house and fill it with gravel to stop rainwater splashing the wall above the DPC.

Installing a chemical damp-proof course

Inserting a new membrane between courses of brickwork or masonry is really a job for a professional. The best DIY solution is to install a chemical DPC. This consists of a silicone-based water-repellent fluid that is injected into the masonry until it is saturated. It then becomes impervious to water and acts as a damp-proof barrier.

DPC injection machines can be hired from most tool hire shops. The shop will supply the injection fluid, power drill and masonry drill bits of the right length and diameter. Ask for an instruction leaflet when you hire the machine, and get advice on the amount of fluid required. You will need roughly 3 litres per metre of wall.

To minimise disruption to the house, the injection process is carried out entirely from the outside of the building.

Tools *Heavy-duty hammer-action power drill; masonry drill bits with depth stop; extension lead and plug-in RCD; safety goggles; work gloves; face mask; damp-proof injection machine.*

Materials *Injection fluid; paraffin for cleaning machine; mortar.*

1 Drill a horizontal row of holes 75mm deep into the course of bricks or stones immediately above the existing DPC. Use a depth stop or mark the bit with tape to ensure that you drill to the correct depth. Space the holes about 120mm apart – two into each stretcher (side-on brick) and one into every header (end-on brick, only found in solid walls). If the bricks are extremely difficult to drill through – or if the walls are made of stone – make the holes in the mortar joints.

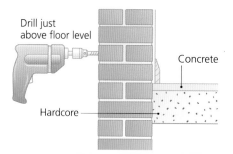

Drill just above floor level

Concrete

Hardcore

With a concrete floor, drill just above it (see above). With a suspended timber floor, drill just below it. For cavity walls, just drill into the outer leaf.

2 When all the holes have been drilled, inject the damp-proofing fluid into them. Follow the instructions supplied with the machine.

Most damp-proof injection machines consist of a pump, a suction nozzle and six injecting nozzles.

3 Insert all but one of the short injection nozzles into the prepared holes and tighten the wing nuts to hold them in place.

4 Hold the free nozzle over the container and turn on the pump. When fluid begins to ooze from the nozzle, turn off the pump.

5 Insert the free nozzle into a hole and tighten its wing nut. Turn on the pump. When the bricks or stones joints are saturated, fluid will 'sweat' from the surface. As soon as this happens, turn off the pump and close the nozzles.

6 Undo the wing nuts, move the nozzles to the next set of holes and repeat the procedure. Continue until you have treated every affected wall.

7 On solid walls, drill through the original holes to a new depth of 150mm. Repeat the treatment cycle, this time using the longer nozzles supplied with the machine.

8 On cavity walls, drill through the original holes into the inner leaf to a total depth of 200mm. Repeat the injection process.

9 When you have finished, empty the machine and clean it with paraffin.

10 Wait for the fluid to dry; it may take two days or more. When the injected course is the same colour as the rest of the wall, fill the holes with mortar.

Windows

Old and rotting windows are a major turn-off for purchasers, who may be reluctant to take on the job of repair or replacement.

Window frames

Window frames are built into the house walls in much the same way as an external door. Modern windows are positioned so that the frame is set back from the face of the masonry by only about 25mm – a fact that contributes to the often short life of wooden casement windows compared with Victorian sash windows. These were set back so that the inside of the frame was flush with the internal wall surface, and as a result the frame was much less exposed to the weather. In areas of the country rated as having severe weather exposure (mainly Scotland and Northern Ireland), Building Regulations require windows to be recessed for this very reason.

Wood is still the most popular material for making window frames. Modern high-performance hardwood windows treated with microporous paints or stains offer excellent durability, and their integral draught-stripping ensures efficient weatherproofing. Cheaper softwood windows need more regular maintenance, but they are the lowest cost choice for new or replacement work.

Steel windows were briefly popular during the 1930s and 1940s, but suffered severely from rust even when they were galvanised. Aluminium windows took their place by the 1960s, creating a trend for uncluttered picture windows. They tended to weather badly, and needed a timber sub-frame because the metal frames were not very strong. They endured for some years in patio door format, but even here other materials have now taken their place.

Plastic (uPVC) windows offer a unique combination of comfort and warmth with a promise of being virtually maintenance-free. They are less widely used in new work, because they are more expensive to specify and their looks are not as aesthetically pleasing as a well-proportioned wooden window. Their longevity is not yet proven.

Casement windows

The casement window is the most widely used type in modern housing. Individual casements may contain glazing bars and a number of smaller panes of glass, rather than a single large pane – styles known generally as cottage (four panes) or Georgian (six or eight panes). Casements are held closed by a simple handle and wedge, and held in an open position with a casement stay and peg.

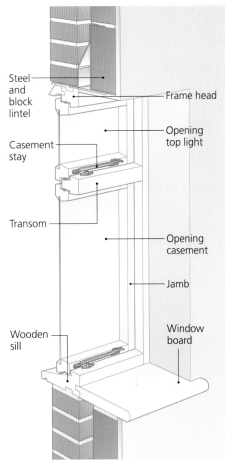

Steel and block lintel

Casement stay

Transom

Wooden sill

Frame head

Opening top light

Opening casement

Jamb

Window board

A casement frame consists of a head, two side jambs and a sill. These components, and any mullions and transoms, are joined with mortise and tenon joints. To help to prevent rain penetration round the opening casements and top ventilators, drip grooves are machined round the inner faces of the frames, mullions and transoms. There are additional grooves round the edges of casements and top ventilators. On high-performance windows, integral weatherstripping is also fitted to make the opening parts of the window weatherproof.

In new buildings, casement frames are usually built into the walls as they rise, and are secured with galvanised ties screwed to the frame and anchored in the mortar courses. Replacement windows are generally secured at the sides by screws and wallplugs or nailable frame fixings.

Sash windows

The sash window was the favoured window style in homes until early in the 20th century. It is a highly complex construction, built into the inner face of the house wall in a rebate in the masonry. This contains the concealed channels for the counterweights that balance the two sliding sashes. Because the frame is set back in this way, there is usually a sub-sill of stone or quarry tiles on which the frame sill rests.

The window frame consists of a head, a sill and two jambs. Each jamb is a vertical box, consisting of an outer lining, a pulley stile, an inner lining and a back lining. A moulding called the parting bead is pinned down the centre of the visible face of the pulley stile. This forms a track between it and the projecting lip of the outer lining to form a vertical track in which the outer (top) sash slides. A second moulding called the staff bead is fixed down the inner edge of the pulley stile to create a parallel track for the inner (bottom) sash.

Near the top of each track, a pulley is fitted into a slot in each pulley stile. This allows the sash cords that connect each

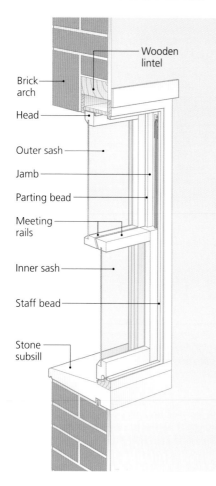

Wooden
lintel

Brick
arch

Head

Outer sash

Jamb

Parting bead

Meeting
rails

Inner sash

Staff bead

Stone
subsill

THE TROUBLE WITH WINDOWS

The commonest problem with all wooden windows is rot. It can attack the frame, its casements or sashes at the joints if water is able to penetrate, and at any point where the glazing putty fails.

Casements can bind or stick in their frames, much as a door does, making them difficult to open and close. Hinges can be damaged if the casement is allowed to swing open violently or any weight is put on it.

Sashes can bind against the pulley stiles, rattle in high winds and let in draughts. However, their biggest problem is failed sash cords, which can be tricky and time-consuming to replace.

Lastly, glass in any window may be cracked or broken by an impact, or by the window slamming shut.

What to do
The most important thing you can do to give your windows the longest life is to maintain them regularly (see page 27). It is failed paintwork that allows rot to gain an initial foothold in window woodwork.

You can carry out most of the everyday repairs a window might need yourself (see pages 21–25). Replacing a window is a major undertaking and you may prefer to leave this to a professional carpenter or builder.

Draughtproofing of casements and sashes can prevent rattling and will cut down on the amount of noise that comes in (see page 115).

sash to its weights to run in and out of the weight compartments as the sashes are raised and lowered. At the bottom of each track a removable cut-out pocket gives access to the weight compartments.

The sashes are square or rectangular frames, sometimes sub-divided by glazing bars into two, four or six smaller panes. A catch on the meeting rails allows the windows to be secured in the closed position.

The modern version of the sliding sash window replaces the cords and weights with spring-loaded spiral balances mounted on the faces of the frame sides. Each sash is attached to its two spiral balances by fixing plates at its bottom corners.

Repairing rot with wood-repair products

There are various products on the market designed to help you to repair rot in a wooden window frame.

Before you start Make sure the item you are repairing is made of painted wood – because the repair will show up on stained or varnished wood.

Tools *Old chisel, about 13mm wide; paint scraper; hot-air gun; paintbrush for applying wood hardener; filling knife; power drill; 10mm twist drill bit; hand or power sander; paintbrush for applying finishing coats to the window.*

Materials *Liquid wood hardener, wood preservative pellets and high-performance wood filler; clear wood preservative; primer, undercoat and gloss paint.*

1 Use a hot-air gun or chemical paint stripper to soften old paint, then scrape it off to reveal the extent of the rotten wood.

2 Dig away the worst of the rot with an old chisel. There is no need to cut back right into sound timber.

3 If the timber is wet it must be dried out. Saturated wood can be covered with a flap of plastic, taped along the top, so that it dries out naturally over a couple of weeks. If it is only damp, dry it rapidly with a hot-air gun. Take care to keep the air flow away from the glass, or you might crack it.

4 When the wood is thoroughly dry, flood the rotten area with brush-loads of wood hardener. The liquid penetrates the wood, and hardens it as it dries, to give a firm base for the filler. Pay particular attention to exposed end grain. Keep flooding on the hardener until it stops soaking readily into the wood and begins to stay on the surface. Let it harden overnight.

5 Mix a small amount of the high-performance wood filler according to the instructions on the container and apply it as quickly as you can to the hole. The filler will start to harden in about five minutes – even quicker in hot weather.

6 Fill in deep cavities with a succession of layers. The filler hardens quickly, so even deep holes can be filled in a short time.

7 Leave the surface of the filled hole as level as you can. After about 30 minutes it can be smoothed level with the surrounding wood with a hand or power sander. This will show up any areas where the filler is still too low.

8 Wipe away the dust and apply more filler, sanding down again afterwards so that the surface is level and smooth.

9 Drill 10mm holes about 20mm deep and 50mm apart in the wood around the repair.

10 Push one of the wood preservative pellets into each hole and then seal it with the wood filler. While the wood is dry, the pellets will remain inactive, but as soon as it becomes wet the pellets will release a fungicide which will prevent wood rot.

11 Coat any bare wood with clear wood preservative.

12 Paint the bare wood with primer and undercoat. Then give the whole window at least two coats of exterior gloss paint.

Repairing rot with new wood

The traditional way of repairing rot in a window is to cut back to sound wood and to insert a new piece.

Before you start Wood used for the repair should match original wood in the window if it has a stained or varnished finish.

Replacing a section of sill or frame

Tools *Pencil; combination square; tenon saw or general purpose saw; chisel, about 20mm wide; mallet; vice; power drill and twist drill bits; paintbrush; plane.*

Materials *Wood to suit size of rotten section; clear wood preservative; zinc-plated No. 10 screws about 50mm long; wood dowels (same diameter as screw heads); waterproof wood adhesive; paint, varnish or preservative wood stain.*

1 Mark cutting lines on the frame about 50mm beyond signs of rot. Draw two right-angled lines on the face of the frame and then mark two more lines at about 45° to the face to form a wedge shape.

2 Using the tenon saw or general purpose saw, cut along the lines as far as possible. Brickwork may prevent you from sawing too far into a sill.

3 Complete the cut with a sharp chisel. Try to leave straight flat sides that will form a tight joint with the new wood.

4 Hold the new wood against the gap and mark the edges to give a cutting line.

5 Cut out the new piece and trim it with the saw or a plane until it is a good fit in the cut-out. It is better if its faces stand slightly proud of the surrounding surface.

6 Treat the cut surfaces of the frame and the new wood with clear wood preservative and allow it to dry.

7 Glue the new wood in place, holding it with G-cramps until the glue is dry.

8 Drill pilot and clearance holes for fixing screws, about 125mm apart.

HELPFUL TIP

If the frame is to be finished with paint, it is a good idea to drill holes in the repaired area at 50mm intervals for inserting wood-preservative pellets. See Repairing rot with wood-repair products (page 21).

9 Drill out the holes about 15mm deep to the same diameter as the screw heads so that the heads will be sunk well below the wood surface.

10 Insert the screws and plug the holes with pieces of glued wood dowel. Drive them firmly home with the mallet.

11 Plane the faces of the insert so they are flush with the surrounding surface. Smooth with abrasive paper, and fill any gaps with exterior grade filler.

12 Finish the repair by applying paint, varnish or a preservative wood stain.

Repairing a rotten window edge

Tools *Screwdriver; panel saw; portable workbench; plane; power drill and 6mm twist drill bit; depth stop; paintbrush.*

Materials *Piece of wood to suit the size of the rotten section; clear wood preservative; waterproof wood glue; sash cramps; 6mm dowels; paint, varnish or preservative wood stain.*

1 If the rot is on the edge of an opening casement or sash, remove it so you can work on it on your workbench. A casement window is taken off by unscrewing the hinges from the frame. Seek specialist advice when removing a sash window.

2 Saw off the rotten part by cutting right along the edge. Cut a replacement length of wood that is slightly oversize.

3 Treat the new wood and the cut surface of the window with clear wood preservative and allow it to dry. Put newspaper on the bench, and ventilate the room.

4 Apply glue to the new wood and fix it in position. Hold the repair together with a pair of sash cramps until the glue has set. Wipe away any excess adhesive.

5 Reinforce the repair by drilling through the new and old wood, and driving in glued dowels. Use a 6mm twist drill bit and dowels of the same size. Before drilling, mark the correct depth of the hole on the drill bit with a depth stop, or wrap a piece of coloured adhesive tape round it.

6 When the glue has set, cut off the protruding lengths of dowel and plane the timber to the exact width and thickness of the existing wood.

7 Fill any minor gaps with exterior wood filler. Finish bare wood with paint, varnish or preservative wood stain, depending on how the rest of the window is treated.

Gaps round a window frame

Damp patches on internal walls may be caused by gaps around the window frame. Fill the gaps before rot starts to attack the wooden frame.

Using frame sealant

Cracks up to about 10mm wide can be filled with frame sealant.

Tools *Trimming knife; thin screwdriver; clean rag.*

Materials *Frame sealant and applicator. Perhaps a jar of water.*

1 With a trimming knife, cut the nozzle off the sealant cartridge at an angle to give the necessary width of sealant to fill the gap. Break the foil seal or cut the sealed top of the cartridge.

2 Wipe around the frame with a clean rag, and inject a bead of sealant into the crack all round. The sealant should be placed in the angle between the window frame and the wall.

For neatness, try to inject the sealant in a single run without stopping, except at corners. Release the trigger to stop the flow.

3 If it is necessary to smooth the sealant, use a wet finger.

4 Sealant can be painted once a skin has formed (one to three weeks), but it is not necessary.

Sealing with mortar

If the gap is more than about 10mm wide it should be filled with mortar, which is available in small bags – ideal for jobs of this scale.

Tools *Plant sprayer; small trowel or filling knife; trimming knife; clean rag.*

Materials *Water; mortar; sealant and applicator.*

1 Dampen the crack with water. A plant sprayer is ideal.

2 Press the mortar in place with a small trowel or filling knife, so that it is level with the surface of the brickwork.

3 When the mortar has hardened, which will take two or three days, seal all round the frame with frame sealant as described above.

EXPANDING FOAM FILLER

For large, irregular gaps that are hard to reach, use a can of expanding foam filler. This adheres to most building materials. It is injected by nozzle at any angle, after which it expands in volume, effectively sealing even hidden areas. Once hardened, the foam is heat, cold and water resistant and rot-proof. It can be cut, sanded, plastered or painted.

Problems with metal windows

Old steel windows often rust, so take a close look at any in your property.

If the putty has been dislodged or the glass cracked, first carefully chip out the putty with an old chisel or hacking knife and remove the glass. If the putty is intact, do not remove it.

Rust in old frames

Tools *Paint scraper or small brush, for paint stripper; small cold chisel; hammer; wire brush; safety goggles; small paintbrush; gloves.*

Materials *Rust remover; zinc-based primer; undercoat; gloss paint; white spirit. Possibly paint stripper and epoxy filler.*

1 Scrape off the paint, or remove it with a chemical paint stripper.

2 Using a small cold chisel, chip off as many of the rust flakes as possible. Then wire-brush the frame by hand, or use a wire wheel or wire-cup brush in a power drill. Wear safety goggles and gloves during this part of the job.

3 Brush over the frame to remove dust and loose particles, then fill any holes with epoxy-based filler and allow it to dry.

4 Paint the prepared frame with a coat of rust remover.

5 When the rust remover is dry, apply a zinc-based metal primer, then an undercoat and two coats of gloss paint.

6 If necessary, re-glaze the window, using metal casement putty.

Paint not adhering to galvanising

On new steel frames paint will sometimes flake off the galvanised surface soon after being applied.

1 Remove existing paint with paint stripper to get right back to the galvanising.

2 Rub the frame lightly with fine wet-and-dry abrasive paper, used wet. Wipe it with a clean damp cloth.

3 When it is dry, wipe it with a clean rag soaked in white spirit, then prime with metal primer.

4 Repaint the window frame with an undercoat and gloss paint.

Condensation

Condensation is quite a common problem with metal windows, and in serious or persistent cases it can lead to the surrounding wallpaper or plaster becoming damp. The most effective solution is to fit a replacement window and frame made of timber or plastic.

Windows that are kept permanently closed are particularly susceptible to condensation. Fitting ventilation locks to these windows and keeping them secured slightly ajar will help.

Alternatively fit a secondary double glazing system or install an extractor fan that will help by extracting the moist air from the room.

Wooden windows that stick

If a window will not open or close easily, examine it carefully to discover the cause.

Build-up of paint

Layers of paint that have built up over the years are a common cause of sticking windows.

1 Use a hot-air gun or chemical paint stripper to strip the edge of the window and the frame back to bare wood.

2 Check that there is a clearance gap of about 2mm between the edge of the window and the frame before repainting.

3 If necessary, plane the window edge to give enough clearance. A casement window can be removed by unscrewing the hinges from the frame.

Swollen timber

Damp that has made the timber swell is also a cause of sticking windows.

1 Strip off the paint and either let the timber dry out during fine weather, or dry it quickly with a hot-air gun.

2 When it is dry make sure there is a clearance gap of about 2mm between window and frame. If necessary, plane the edge of the window.

3 Repaint the window, ensuring that putty around the glass is well covered with paint.

Staff beads too tight

On a sliding sash window, the staff beads might have been nailed on too close to the inner sash.

1 Prise off the staff beads and re-nail them so they lightly touch the edges of the inner sash. Before driving the nails right in, test that the sash will slide easily.

2 Rub the inside face of the staff bead with a candle to help to improve the sliding action.

Decorating the outside of a house

Exterior paintwork needs repainting every five years or so. Check the whole exterior from time to time for the first signs of deterioration – when gloss paint loses its shine, or when emulsion becomes over-powdery to the touch.

Before you start Surfaces should be clean, stable, and stripped if the paintwork is not sound. Repair damaged areas of a rendered wall and fix gutters. Some weeks before you intend to start painting, check that putty around windows is sound and, if not, replace it.

Before you buy the paint If you are going to change your colour scheme, make sure that the new colours will fit in with the surrounding and neighbouring buildings.

Calculate how much paint you need. Rendered surfaces require more paint than smooth ones. If all the walls are to be painted, estimate the total outside area of the house by multiplying the length of the walls by the height.

If you are going to paint the pipes and the outside of gutters, multiply their circumference in centimetres by their length. Divide this figure by 10,000 to give an area in square metres.

Which paint to use In general, use exterior grade gloss paint on wood and metal – gutters, downpipes, windows and doors – and use exterior grade emulsion or masonry paint on walls.

Alternatively, on bare wood you can use microporous paint, which needs no primer or undercoat. This paint allows trapped air or moisture to evaporate, reducing the risk of flaking associated with hardwoods.

You do not have to use a paint similar to the one previously used, but never put gloss paint over surfaces (mainly pipes and guttering) that are coated with bituminous paint. If you are doubtful about whether old paint contains bitumen, rub a rag soaked with petrol over the surface. If the rag picks up a brownish stain, the paint is bituminous. Either continue to use bituminous paint or, providing the surface is sound, coat it with aluminium primer-sealer, then paint with undercoat and gloss.

Paint the house in this order

Complete all the preparatory work before you do any painting – but never leave a surface exposed. Protect it with at least a primer and, if possible, an undercoat before you stop work at the end of a session.

Always decorate from the top of the house downwards so that the newly painted surfaces cannot be spoilt. Paint doors and windows last. Most professional decorators work in the following order, but if you are working from a scaffold tower you may wish to paint all the surfaces you can reach before moving the tower to another site. Try to keep on painting a wall until you reach a natural break.

1 Bargeboards, fascias and soffits
All these surfaces are painted in the same way, but not necessarily at the same time. Gutters are usually painted the same colour as fascias so it is easiest to paint them immediately afterwards – before soffits, which are often painted to match the walls or windows.
• Apply knotting, if necessary, and primer to bare wood. Put on an undercoat and leave to dry. Use two undercoats if there is to be a colour change.
• Lightly sand with fine abrasive paper to remove any rough bits.
• Apply a coat of gloss with a 75mm paintbrush, finishing with the grain. Leave it to dry for at least 12 hours.
• Apply a second coat of gloss.

2 Gutters and downpipes
Whether you paint gutters and pipes together or at different times, follow the same painting procedure for both.
• Clean out debris and wash with water and detergent.
• Remove rust from the insides of metal gutters with a wire brush. Wipe the surface with a dry cloth and apply rust inhibitor or metal primer. Paint the inside of gutters with any left-over gloss paint.
• Paint gutters and pipes with exterior gloss. If there is to be a colour change, apply one or more undercoats first.
• Hold a piece of cardboard behind pipes as you paint them, to protect the wall.
• Apply a second coat of paint when the first is completely dry.

Plastic gutters and pipes do not have to be painted, but if you want them to match a colour scheme, apply two coats of exterior grade gloss. Do not use a primer or undercoat. Manufacturers usually advise against painting new plastic because the paint will not adhere perfectly to it. After about a year it is safe to do so.

3 House walls

• Treat new rendering which has not been painted before with a stabilising solution or a primer recommended for such a surface by the manufacturer.
• On painted rendering or a textured surface no undercoat is necessary. Apply two coats of exterior grade emulsion or masonry paint with a 100mm or 150mm paintbrush or an exterior grade shaggy pile roller. If you use a brush, work the paint into the surface with the tip of the bristles.
• Paint the area close to door and window frames with a 50mm or 75mm brush.
• Do not try to paint the whole width of a wall along a house in one go. Instead, divide each wall into sections and paint one section at a time. If you cannot finish

Bargeboards
Soffit
Fascia
Gutters
Downpipes
Weatherboarding
Tiled sills
Painted door
House walls
Brick walls

painting a wall in one session, stop at a corner of a feature – a window, for instance – so that joins will be less noticeable. Never stop in the middle of a wall. It will leave a noticeable mark.

4 Brick walls

• Avoid painting good facing brickwork – it is difficult to achieve a satisfactory finish, it cannot be successfully cleaned off later and rarely looks attractive.
• If you really want to paint it, use exterior grade emulsion and a rough surface paintbrush. Apply at least two coats.
• To clean dirty bricks, scrub them with a hard bristle brush and plenty of water.

Never use soap or detergent because they leave permanent white stains.

5 Windows

If a concrete sill is damaged, repair it.
• Strip paint off wooden sills and fill holes and uneven areas with exterior grade wood stopping or epoxy-based filler.
• Apply knotting to knots and resinous patches in bare wood. Then apply primer, undercoat and exterior grade gloss with a 25mm, 50mm or angled cutting-in brush.
• Paint the window frames carefully.
• Take special care to seal the joint between putty and glass with new paint. This will prevent rain seeping through the window.

6 Tiled sills

• Clean window sills made of clay tiles with a fine wire brush; wash away the dirt and dry with a cloth.
• Clay tiles can be painted with special tile paint which is available in a limited colour range. No primer or undercoat is needed. Apply two coats with a 50mm paintbrush.

7 Painted doors

• Remove metal handles and other fixtures before painting.
• Replace any damaged putty in a glass-panelled door.
• Use exterior grade gloss to finish.

8 Varnished weatherboarding

• If the varnish is in good condition, rub over the surface with a flexible sanding pad damped with water to remove the glaze. Wash down with clean water, allow the surface to dry and then apply new varnish.
• If the varnish is in poor condition, strip it. Brush on a wood preservative then varnish.

9 Painted weatherboarding

• Apply knotting, if needed, then wood primer, undercoat and two coats of exterior gloss paint. Alternatively, use microporous paint suitable for exterior woodwork.
• Work from the top down, and from left to right if you are right-handed and from right to left if you are left handed.
• Paint sections about 1m long at a time, using a brush just narrower than the width of one board.
• Paint the edge of the timber first, then paint the face, finishing with strokes that go with the grain.

Pitched roofs

Always check the condition of the roof when viewing a house. Major faults mean big repair bills.

Until around the 1960s, pitched-roof construction was a job for skilled carpenters, who would cut and fix the individual timbers one by one to form the roof structure the house required. Modern houses are built almost exclusively using prefabricated roof trusses, which allow the roof structure to be erected much more quickly and also eliminate the need for internal load-bearing walls in all but the largest properties.

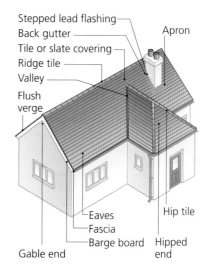

Stepped lead flashing
Back gutter
Apron
Tile or slate covering
Ridge tile
Valley
Flush verge
Eaves
Fascia
Barge board
Gable end
Hip tile
Hipped end

Traditional roof construction

The simplest pitched roof is called a lean-to or mono-pitch roof. It is a slope that usually abuts a wall at its higher end. The roof consists of sloping rafters, resting at each end on a horizontal timber wallplate. It may be installed on single-storey extensions, porches and attached garages and, in the past, was often used to roof the additions at the rear of Victorian terraces.

The span of a pitched roof can be increased by butting two mono-pitch roofs together to form a so-called double-pitch roof. The two roof slopes meet at a ridge board, and the bottom ends of the rafters forming each slope are tied together by joists to create a rigid triangular structure. Gable walls fill in the open ends of the roof. This type of roof structure is limited in

span to about 4m, and is found mainly in terraced housing. If the house has an internal loadbearing wall, struts can be added between the purlins and a wallplate resting on top of the internal wall. The addition of a collar tie between the rafters at the level of the purlins creates a roof structure that can comfortably span the width of most houses.

A duo-pitch roof may have sloping ends (called hips) instead of gables. Each hip is formed by two diagonal hip rafters that support the end of the ridge board, and short jack rafters are fitted between the hip rafters and the wallplates to complete the roof structure.

Where two duo-pitched roofs meet in an L-shape, they form an external hip and an internal valley, which is supported by a valley rafter and jack rafters in the same way as a hip is formed. The valley is either lined with a lead gutter or with specially shaped valley tiles.

Ridge board
Purlin
Wall plate
Common rafter
Binder
Hanger
Joist
Loadbearing internal wall
Strut

Purlin roof The commonest type of duo-pitch roof is the purlin roof. This has a horizontal beam called a purlin running between the gable ends along each slope of the roof, midway between the ridge board and the eaves, to provide extra support for the rafters. This increases the unsupported span of the roof to about 7m.

Prefabricated roofs

Almost all modern (post 1960s) house roofs are built using roof trusses, which are prefabricated in a variety of shapes to cater for most roof designs. Each roof truss combines rafters, joists and struts in a W-pattern to create a frame that is extremely strong and can span the external walls of the building with no need for internal load-bearing walls. The triangular structure does not deform under load, so the timbers used can be slimmer in cross-section than those in a traditional roof. This has the advantages of lower cost, lighter weight and ease of handling on site.

The components of each roof truss are butt-jointed and fixed together with galvanised steel connector plates. They are positioned at 600mm centres on wallplates at each side of the span, and are nailed into place. There is no ridge board, but the row of trusses has to be braced to prevent it from collapsing sideways. Horizontal braces are fitted where the W-shaped internal supports meet the rafters and the ceiling joists, and diagonal braces are added across the underside of each section of the roof slope, running from the ridge to the eaves. The roof structure is tied to the house walls with galvanised steel straps to prevent the roof from lifting or gable walls collapsing in high winds.

Trussed rafter
Bracing
Wall plate

Roof coverings

Pitched roofs are traditionally covered with tiles or slates. Other materials such as split stone and thatch are found in localised areas of the country. Their installation, maintenance and repair are best left to specialist contractors.

In older houses, the roof covering is laid on closely spaced horizontal battens nailed across the upper edges of the rafters. In old roofs, this method allowed fine rain and snow to blow through the gaps between the tiles or slates and into the roof space. This was prevented by trowelling a mixture of mortar and animal hair into the gaps from inside the roof (a process called torching) or by boarding the roof slope. Since the 1930s it has been usual to lay underfelt (called sarking) over the rafters before the battens are fixed.

Slates and plain tiles

There are always two layers of tile or slate at any point on the roof, and three layers directly over each batten. This double-lapping prevents the water running off one tile or slate from entering the roof space through the gap between the tile or slate in the course below. Slates are nailed to the battens at every course. Plain tiles have nibs on the back which hook over the roof battens, and are usually nailed only at every third or fourth course.

Other types of tile, such as traditional pantiles and large modern concrete tiles, overlap or interlock with their neighbours in each course. This prevents rain penetrating between their edges, so they can be laid

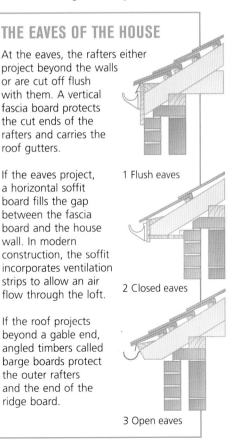

THE EAVES OF THE HOUSE

At the eaves, the rafters either project beyond the walls or are cut off flush with them. A vertical fascia board protects the cut ends of the rafters and carries the roof gutters.

If the eaves project, a horizontal soffit board fills the gap between the fascia board and the house wall. In modern construction, the soffit incorporates ventilation strips to allow an air flow through the loft.

1 Flush eaves

2 Closed eaves

If the roof projects beyond a gable end, angled timbers called barge boards protect the outer rafters and the end of the ridge board.

3 Open eaves

with a single lap. This saves on both labour and materials when covering the roof. Tiles are fixed to the battens with nails or, more commonly on modern roofs, with side-fixing clips. Usually every third course is fixed, plus all perimeter tiles.

Flashings
Where a roof slope meets a wall or a chimney stack, flashings make the join waterproof. Lead, zinc, copper and mortar have been used, but lead is the most common material. It is cut into strips that are let into the mortar joints of the wall and shaped to overlap the roof covering.

Chimney stacks

The exposed part of the chimney stack can suffer from failed pointing and flaunching, loose chimney pots, damage to brickwork and to the flashings. Check the state of the chimney stack regularly, especially after high winds, so that faults can be rectified before they become serious. Unless you are experienced in working at heights, it is best to leave chimney stack repairs to a professional builder.

THE TROUBLE WITH ROOFS

A well-built pitched roof will last for decades (or longer), but several problems are commonplace. Individual slates and tiles can slip out of position, allowing water to penetrate the roof structure, and ridge and hip tiles can be dislodged by high winds if their mortar bedding fails. Slates can become brittle with age, and both tiles and slates can be damaged by careless roofing contractors or reckless householders climbing on the roof surface. Metal flashings can be torn or lifted by high winds, and mortar flashings may crack and fall out.

What to do
Unless you have the proper access equipment and are experienced in working at heights, it is safest to leave all roofing work to professionals. You may be able to carry out minor repairs close to the eaves via a ladder. If you feel you are capable of carrying out work on the roof slope, you can replace tiles and slates (see pages 30–37) and repair flashings (pages 38–39).

Roof repairs

Missing or broken slates or tiles can quickly become a problem, allowing water to penetrate the roof space and wind to lift more of the neighbouring tiles. Act promptly to fix the problem.

Making a temporary repair to a cracked tile or slate

If rainwater is coming in through a cracked tile or slate and it is not possible to get a replacement immediately, you can use flashing strip to make a temporary repair to minimise the damage done by damp. Alternatively, bituminous sealant in an applicator gun seals a fine crack with very little work: prop up the surrounding tiles and brush the crack as for flashing strip (below), and then inject the sealant.

Tools *Ladder with a stand-off bracket; roof ladder; wooden wedges (see box, right); wire brush; paintbrush; sharp knife; old wallpaper seam roller.*

Materials *Flashing strip primer; self-adhesive flashing strip.*

---

1 Raise the one or two tiles or slates that overlap the cracked one, to give you better access. Prop them up with small wooden wedges (see right). Use the wire brush to clean the surface round the crack.

2 Brush a coat of flashing strip primer into and round the crack, making a strip as wide as the flashing strip. The primer ensures a good bond between tile or slate and flashing strip.

3 Cut a piece of flashing strip from the roll with a sharp knife. Make it long enough to cover the whole crack.

4 Press the strip into place and bed it down well. Run a small wallpaper seam roller to and fro over it to firm it down.

Replacing a broken plain tile

If you don't have a spare tile of the same size and style as the broken one, a builders' yard or salvage merchant may have one.

Before you start Beware of matching the replacement tile to the colour your tiles were when new. The tiles may have changed colour considerably, so try to match the replacement to the colour they are now. If you can't find a good match, 'steal' a tile from an unobtrusive place on the roof – such as a side porch. Put the poor match in its place.

Tools *Ladder with stand-off bracket; roof ladder; wooden wedges; large builder's trowel. Perhaps a slate ripper.*

Materials *Replacement tile.*

WEDGES TO PROP TILES UP

To prop up tiles you need to prepare two or more wedges from 20mm thick wood. Cut them 200mm long and make them taper from 30mm at one end to a point at the other.

1 Lift the two tiles that overlap the broken tile from the course above. Tap a wooden wedge under each to hold it up.

2 Slip the large builder's trowel under the broken tile. Lift up the whole tile until its nibs are clear of the batten and you can draw it out towards you. If the broken tile has been nailed to the batten, free it by wiggling it from side to side until the nail breaks or comes away. If this does not free it, you will need a slate ripper to cut through the nails.

3 Lay the replacement tile on the trowel and slide it up under the two wedged tiles until the nibs hook over the batten. There is no need to nail it, even if the original was nailed. Take out the wedges.

Replacing a group of plain tiles

If you need to replace a group of tiles and have no spares, buy replacements of the same size and style.

Tools *Ladder with stand-off bracket; roof ladder; wooden wedges (left); large builder's trowel; claw hammer; bucket on a long rope. Perhaps a slate ripper.*

Materials *Replacement tiles; 40mm aluminium-alloy roofing nails.*

1 Lift the tiles in the course immediately above the highest ones to be replaced. Tiles are hung with their joints staggered from row to row. Lift them two at a time and slide the wooden wedges under their outer edges to hold them up. This will allow you access to the single tile they overlap in the course below.

2 As each tile is exposed, slide the trowel under it and lift it until its nibs clear the batten. Then draw it out. Lower it to the ground in the bucket.

3 Work along the top course of tiles to be removed and then along the course below that, and so on until all the tiles have been removed. Once the highest course of tiles has been removed, you can lift the others without using the wedges or the trowel.

4 Fit the replacement tiles onto the battens along the bottom course first. Hook each tile over the batten by its nibs and make sure that it is centred over the gap between the two tiles below it. Then work along the courses above.

5 Nail each tile in every third or fourth course to the batten with two nails.

Replacing broken single lap tiles

Tools *Ladder with a stand-off bracket; roof ladder; wooden wedges (page 31). Perhaps a slate ripper; hammer; bucket on a rope.*

Materials *Replacement tiles. Perhaps tile clips and 40mm roofing aluminium-alloy roofing nails.*

1 Slide up the tiles that overlap onto the broken tile. Alternatively, use wedges to raise the tiles to the left and right of the broken one, but in the course above.

2 To remove the broken tile, tilt it sideways to separate it from the tiles that are interlocked with it. You will be able to free it without disturbing them. Lever the tile upwards to release it from any clip that holds it to the batten. If the clip stays in place, the new tile may slip into it. If the clip is dislodged, there is no need to replace it; a few unclipped tiles will not matter. Sometimes alternate courses are nailed in place. If your repair is to a nailed tile, use a slate ripper to cut the nails before you remove the tile.

3 Lower the broken tile in a bucket on a rope to a helper on the ground.

4 To fit the replacement tile, slide it up into place. You will not be able to nail it or clip it. Pull back into place any tiles that you pushed out of place. Remove any wedges.

Replacing a group of tiles

Remove the highest tiles as for a single tile. Lower tiles simply need tilting to free them. Remove the clips wherever you can.

When replacing the tiles, fit the lowest course first and work from right to left.

Fit a clip for each tile wherever you are able to nail it to the batten.

Lodge the hook of the clip over the ridge at the side of the tile and hammer the nail through the hole in the clip into the top edge of the batten near the bottom edge of the tile you are fitting.

You can also nail alternate courses to the battens. The highest course cannot be nailed and the last tile of all cannot be fitted with a clip because the batten will be covered.

Making repairs to slate roofs

Slates will last a century or more, but the nails holding them to the battens can corrode and break, allowing the slates to slip out of position.

Before you start The two problems most likely to affect a slate roof are nail-sickness and delamination. Corrosion, or nail-sickness, can affect a large area of a roof within a few years as the nails are the same age and corrode at the same rate. The slates can be re-nailed provided that they are sound.

A more serious problem is delamination, when the surface of the slate becomes flaky or powdery and you can see many cracks and splits. Replacement is the usual solution.

Fixing slates For fixing a group of replacement slates in several courses you can use 40mm aluminium-alloy or copper roofing nails. If these are hard to find and you only have a small group of slates to nail into place, 40mm large-head galvanised clout nails will do.

When replacing single slates, you will not be able to nail them because the batten will be covered by the course of slates above. You can secure each slate with a strip of metal cut from lead, zinc, or aluminium that is thin enough to bend. It is fixed between the slates (see opposite). Slates can also be fixed with expanding foam, applied under a loose slate from outside or inside the loft.

CUTTING A SLATE TO SIZE

Place the slate on a flat board and use a ceramic tile cutter and a metal rule to score a deep cutting line. To complete the cut, use a wide bolster chisel. Tap it gently along the scored line with a hammer. Or you can place the slate on a table with the scored line over the table edge and press down to break the slate cleanly.

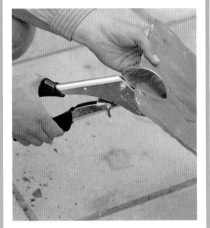

If you have many slates to cut, hire a slate cutter. Cut with the top surface of the slate downwards. On a secondhand slate in particular this ensures that weathering and cutting marks match the other slates.

How to make holes New slates will not have fixing holes in them; you will have to make the holes.

A secondhand slate may have its holes in the wrong place and need drilling. Use the old slate as a pattern to mark drilling spots. The holes are usually about half-way down the sides.

Drill the holes with an electric drill fitted with a No. 6 masonry bit; or make the hole by tapping a nail through the slate with steady, not-too-hard hammer blows.

Work from the underside, that is the side without the bevelled edges.

Replacing a broken slate

Slates may become cracked with age, or by someone clambering on the roof without using proper access equipment. You may not be able to obtain a matching replacement slate immediately. If so, make a temporary repair to prevent water from penetrating (see page 30). Alternatively, you can coat the slate with mastic. Cover this with a piece of roofing felt or cooking foil cut to fit and spread another layer of mastic on top. Replace the slate when you can obtain one that is a good match.

Tools *Ladder with a stand-off bracket; roof ladder; slate ripper; a bucket on a long rope; hammer or screwdriver. Perhaps a power drill fitted with No. 6 masonry bit, or nail and hammer.*

Materials *Replacement slate; strip of lead, zinc, aluminium or copper 25mm wide, and long enough to reach from the hole in the slate to the bottom plus 100mm; 40mm large-head galvanised clout nails.*

1 Cut through the nails that are holding the slate, using the slate ripper.

2 Draw the slate towards you, wiggling it from side to side to ease it from under the slates overlapping it. Take care not to let any broken pieces slide off the roof. They are sharp and can cause damage or injury. Put the pieces in a bucket and take it to the ground or lower it down to a helper.

3 Nail the metal strip to the batten, which will just be visible in the gap between the two slates the replacement is going to lap onto. Put the nail in a ready-made hole about 25mm down from the top of the strip.

4 Carry the new slate up to the roof in a bucket or put it into a bucket and haul it up with a rope.

5 Slip the new slate, with bevelled edges upwards, under the two slates in the course above. Wiggle it a little to right and left to work it upwards until its lower edge aligns with the slates on each side. Its top edge will fit tightly over the batten to which the course above is nailed.

6 Turn up the end of the metal strip over the lower edge of the slate, then bend it double and press it down flat against the slate. The double thickness prevents snow and ice from forcing the clip open.

Replacing a group of slates

You will be able to nail the lower courses of slates in place, but the top course and the course below that will have to be fixed with metal strips because the battens to which they should be nailed will be covered by slates (see Replacing a broken slate, page 33). If necessary, cut the slates to size and drill holes in them.

Tools *Ladder with a stand-off bracket; roof ladder; slate ripper; hammer; a bucket on a long rope; screwdriver.*

Materials *Replacement slates; 40mm aluminium-alloy or copper roofing nails; strips of lead, zinc, aluminium or copper 25mm wide and long enough to reach from the hole in the slate to the bottom plus 100mm.*

1 Cut through the nails securing the damaged slates, using a slate ripper. Deal first with the highest course to be removed. Ease each slate out in turn from the

overlapping slates and lower it in a bucket to a helper or take it to the ground. Do not let a slate slide from the roof; it is sharp and can cause damage or injury.

Work down course by course, removing the slates. The lower ones will not be overlapped and are easier to remove.

2 Fix the bottom course of replacement slates first. Butt neighbouring slates closely and fit them with the bevelled edges upwards. Nail the slates through the holes to the batten.

3 Work upwards, course by course, nailing the slates in place. When you can no longer see the battens to nail the slates to, cut metal strips to secure the slates and fit them as described in Replacing a broken slate (page 33).

Replacing ridge, hip and bonnet tiles

Both tiled and slate roofs have the gaps at the ridge and hips covered by specially designed tiles. The tiles are most often curved, but may be angled.

Replacing a bonnet hip tile
Some tiled roofs have bonnet hip tiles to cover the gap at the hip. Bonnet hip tiles are nailed to the hip timber as well as being bedded in mortar.

1 Remove a bonnet hip tile by chipping away the mortar above and below it with a cold chisel and club hammer and then sliding a slate ripper under the tile and giving a sharp hammer blow on the handle to cut through the nail. You can then draw out the tile towards you.

2 If you are removing several tiles down the hip, start at the highest one and work downwards. Clean the tiles of old mortar.

3 Brush away all dust from around the repair, then brush the area with water and with PVA adhesive.

4 If you are replacing a single tile, spread mortar to bed it on. Spread mortar also under the bonnet in the course above. Set the bonnet in place and tap it into alignment with the other tiles in the course before you smooth the mortar and clean away any excess.

5 If you are replacing several bonnets, work from the bottom upwards. Nail each, except the top one, to the timber with an aluminium nail after you have set it on the mortar. Then smooth the mortar and clean away any excess.

Replacing ridge or hip tiles

The most common problem at the roof ridge or hip is that the mortar between tiles cracks and crumbles away. Sometimes a tile may then be pushed out of place by a build-up of ice, or occasionally by strong winds. If you spot cracks early, while they are narrow, you can fill them with roof-and-gutter sealant. There are coloured sealants which make the repair scarcely noticeable.

If the mortar is crumbling or the tile itself has cracked, you will have to remove the tile and re-fix it or put a new one in its place. If it is the end ridge tile that needs a repair, you must seal up the opening left at the end. Use small pieces of slate or tile bedded in mortar. If the main roof tiles are S-shaped there will be a hollow to seal where the ridge or hip tile meets them.

Tools *Ladder with a stand-off bracket; roof ladder; cold chisel; club hammer; brush; paintbrush; small builder's trowel.*

Materials *Dry mortar mix, or cement and sharp sand; PVA adhesive; bucket of water. Perhaps replacement tiles, narrow pieces of tile or slate.*

1 With the chisel and hammer, carefully chip away all cracked or crumbling mortar until the ridge or hip tile is freed and you can lift it off. Make sure that any surrounding mortar you leave in place is sound. Clean the tile.

2 Prepare the mortar from a bag of dry mixed material or make your own from one part cement to four parts sharp sand. To improve adhesion, add some PVA adhesive to the water, following the manufacturer's instructions. Do not make the mortar too wet; a firmer mix is easier to work with. Mix enough to half-fill a bucket.

3 Brush all dust away from the area round the repair.

4 Use the paintbrush and water to wet the roof and the existing mortar round the repair. This is especially necessary on a hot day when the mortar would lose its moisture too quickly and crack.

5 Brush PVA adhesive liberally all round the area of the repair to ensure good adhesion between the roof tiles at the ridge or hip and the ridge or hip tile itself.

6 Use the trowel to spread mortar on the roof on both sides of the ridge or hip. Cover the areas where the bottom edges of the tile to be fixed will lie.

Do not use too much mortar; there must be a gap under the ridge or hip tiles so that air can circulate to keep the timber below dry. If you lay too much mortar on the tiles, it could squeeze into the gap and fill it in when you are setting the ridge or hip tile into place.

7 The butt joints where two of the ridge or hip tiles meet can either be pointed with mortar or given a solid bedding of mortar. It is probably best to follow the method already used on the roof.

If you make a solid bedding, place a piece of slate or tile across the gap between the two sides of the ridge or hip to prevent mortar falling through.

8 Ridge or hip tiles must be dipped in water before they are set in place. Do this before you go up on the roof. Settle the tile on the mortar carefully so that it makes a smooth line with the neighbouring tiles.

Alternatively If the roof tiles have a curved profile, fill the gap between the down-curve and the ridge or hip tiles with pieces of tile or slate embedded in mortar.

Specially designed 'dentil slips' can be bought for this purpose.

9 Smooth the mortar between tiles and along the bottom edges. There must be no hollows in the mortar between the tiles because they could retain small pockets of rainwater.

10 If the re-fixed tile is at an end of the roof ridge, seal the open end with thin slips of tile or slate bedded in mortar. Smooth the end so that rainwater will flow off readily.

11 If you have been replacing the lowest tile on the hip, make sure the protecting hip iron has not been dislodged; remake its fixings if necessary. Then fill the end of the tile with mortar.

Repairs to verges

A roof with only two main slopes is usually sealed with mortar where the slopes meet the gable ends of the house – these are the verges.

Before you start You can seal any minor cracks in the mortar with roof-and-gutter sealant injected with an applicator gun.

If you choose a sealant to match the mortar, the repair will not be noticeable. For larger cracks you will have to make the repair with mortar.

Tools *Ladder with a stand-off bracket; cold chisel; club hammer; brush; paintbrush; small trowel.*

Materials *Dry mortar mix, or cement and sharp sand; PVA adhesive; bucket of water. Perhaps narrow slips of tile.*

1 With the chisel and hammer, chip away all cracked and crumbling mortar, leaving only sound mortar in place.

2 Prepare the mortar from a bag of dry mixed material or from one part cement to four parts sharp sand. To improve adhesion, add PVA adhesive to the water, following the manufacturer's instructions. Avoid making the mixture too wet. Make enough mortar to half-fill a bucket.

3 Brush all dust away, then dampen the area with some water using a paintbrush before brushing on a covering of PVA adhesive.

4 Use the trowel to press the mortar firmly into the areas that have been prepared. Knock it in with the side of the trowel to make sure that there are no pockets of air in it.

5 Smooth the surface of the mortar and clean away any excess. Do not leave any ledges or hollows in the mortar that could retain rainwater.

Repairs to metal valleys

Where two roof slopes meet at the bottom, the long narrow gap between them is sealed – frequently by a tray of aluminium alloy, lead or zinc. This metal valley is overlapped by the tiles or slates, which drain rainwater into it to be carried down to the gutters at the eaves.

Since valleys are likely to carry a gushing stream of water in heavy rain, they must be kept waterproof and clear of obstructions. If moss, leaves or other debris accumulates, rainwater will build up at the obstruction and spill over the edges of the valley onto the timbers and into the roof space.

If a metal valley has developed a fine crack or is showing the first signs of corrosion, it can be repaired with a liquid bitumen compound. Liquid bitumen can also be used to make a temporary repair if you are waiting for a convenient time to replace the valley.

Holes or splits in a metal valley can be covered with a self-adhesive metal-backed flashing strip. If slight corrosion has set in over a large area, flashing strip can be used to cover the entire valley.

Repairing with liquid bitumen

Stir the waterproofing compound before you apply it. You can use it on a damp, but not wet, surface. Do not use it, however, if rain or frost are expected within 24 hours.

Tools *Ladder with a stand-off bracket; roof ladder; wire brush; a spreader for the roof-and-gutter sealant; sharp knife or scissors; soft brush or broom.*

Materials *Roof-and-gutter sealant; roofing felt or cooking foil; liquid bitumen waterproofing compound; bucket of water.*

1 Use the wire brush to clean away dirt and loose metal fragments from the area of the valley that is going to be repaired.

2 Spread roof-and-gutter sealant over the damaged area and at least 50mm beyond it.

3 Cut out a piece of roofing felt or cooking foil to cover the damage and extend at least 50mm beyond it. Press the felt or foil down over the sealant.

4 Spread another layer of sealant on top of the felt or foil.

5 Brush the liquid bitumen waterproofing compound over the repair. As a precaution against leaks, you can brush it over the whole valley. Apply it with a soft brush or broom, dipping the brush in water and shaking it each time before you load it with the waterproofer. Brush the compound on with even strokes, working in the same direction all the time. Throw the brush away when you have finished.

Making repairs with flashing strip

Tools *Ladder with a stand-off bracket; roof ladder; wire brush; damp cloth; paintbrush; sharp knife or strong scissors; old wallpaper seam roller.*

Materials *Medium-coarse abrasive paper; flashing-strip primer; self-adhesive metal-backed flashing strip.*

1 Use the wire brush to clean away dirt and loose metal fragments from round the crack or hole.

2 Rub over the area with abrasive paper.

3 Wipe the surface clean with the damp cloth and allow it to dry completely.

4 Use the paintbrush to apply a coat of flashing-strip primer to the area of the repair, extending it at least 50mm beyond the damage. Leave it to dry for the time recommended by the manufacturer – usually about 30 minutes.

5 Cut out a piece of flashing strip to extend at least 50mm beyond the crack or hole all round. Cut it with a knife or pair of scissors, then peel off the backing.

6 Press the flashing strip firmly into position, using the wallpaper seam roller to bed it down smoothly.

Repairs to flashings

Where a tile or slate roof meets a wall, there is a flashing to seal the join – for example at the meeting of a roof with a chimney stack and the meeting of a bay window or porch roof with the house wall.

Flashings fitted when the house is built are usually strips of lead which can deteriorate with age. Depending on the extent of the deterioration, it may not be necessary to replace the flashing. Small repairs are quite easily achieved.

Fine cracks To repair a fine crack, inject some bituminous sealant or other roof-and-gutter sealant into it with an applicator gun and cartridge. Some sealants are available in different colours so you can choose one that will make the repair less noticeable.

Small holes or slight corrosion A patch of self-adhesive flashing strip will make a sound repair over a small hole or where there are the first signs of corrosion.

Use the method described for a roof valley under Making repairs with flashing strip (left).

Renewing flashing mortar The top edge of a flashing is sandwiched into the mortar between two courses of bricks. Sometimes it works loose and lets in water.

Repoint the joint (page 14), but first push the edge of the flashing back into the gap between courses of bricks.

If the flashing springs out, wedge it with blocks of wood until the pointing has hardened. Then withdraw the blocks and fill the holes with mortar.

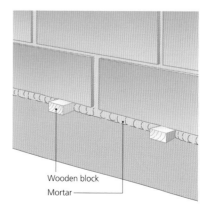

Wooden block

Mortar

Replacing a flashing

If a flashing is badly cracked or corroded, replace it with a self-adhesive metal-backed flashing strip. Unlike lead flashing, adhesive flashing is not tucked into the mortar joints.

Tools *Ladder with a stand-off bracket; roof ladder; plugging chisel and club hammer; pointing trowel; wire brush; paintbrush; sharp craft knife; old wallpaper seam roller.*

Materials *Mortar for repointing (page 14); flashing-strip primer; self-adhesive metal-backed flashing-strip.*

1 Chip out any mortar that is still holding the flashing in the joints between bricks or masonry. Use the plugging chisel and hammer. Protect your hands and eyes.

2 Strip away the old flashing.

3 Use the wire brush to clean away loose mortar and dirt from the area to be repaired.

4 Repoint the joints between the courses of bricks or masonry (page 14). Let the new pointing dry out overnight.

5 Paint a coat of flashing primer on the wall (or chimney) and roof where the strip is to go. Let it dry for 30 minutes to an hour, according to the manufacturer's instructions.

6 Cut two lengths of flashing strip, each the full length of the area to be sealed.

7 Peel off the backing of the first strip and put the strip in position, letting the width lie equally on the roof and the wall (or chimney stack). Roll the strip with the wallpaper seam roller to smooth it out and ensure that it is well stuck.

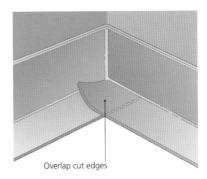

Overlap cut edges

8 At internal corners, make a snip in the lower edge of the strip and overlap the cut edges.

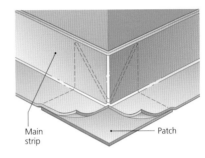

Main strip   Patch

9 At external corners, fit a square patch before the main strip; make a cut from one corner of the patch to the middle. Set the patch with the centre at the point where the wall angle meets the roof and the cut running upwards. Let the cut edges splay out round the angle. In the main strip make a cut in the bottom edge and let the cut edges splay apart over the patch. Trim off any excess at the points.

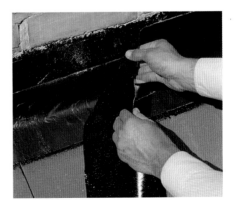

10 Peel the backing off the second strip and apply it so that its top edge is 50mm above the top edge of the first layer. Treat any corners as in the first strip. Again smooth the strip out and bed it down well with the wallpaper seam roller.

Flat roofs

Flat roofs are relatively uncommon on new homes today. In the 1960s and 1970s, every home extension had one because it was cheap and quick to erect.

Poor quality felting on these roofs led to a host of problems, and many owners gave up the constant round of repairs and put on a pitched roof instead. Planners, too, grew disillusioned with flat roofs on domestic buildings and it is now difficult to obtain consent to build anything with a flat roof. Despite this, there are many flat roofs still in existence.

Flat roof construction

A flat roof is not truly horizontal; it needs a slight slope to drain rainwater off its surface. To create the required slope, which should be 1 in 60 for a felted roof, tapered battens called furring strips are fixed to the top edges of the joists. If the roof slope is to run at right angles to the joist direction, the strips also run at right angles to the joists.

The roof decking is nailed in place. It may be tongued-and-grooved softwood boards, roofing-grade chipboard coated with bitumen or exterior-grade plywood.

Roof coverings

There are two materials commonly used on new domestic flat roofs; built-up felt and mastic asphalt. You may find lead, copper or zinc sheet roofs on older properties, especially on flat-topped window bays and porches.

Felt is usually built up in three layers, bonded together with hot or cold bitumen. Felt is available in several types, the cheapest of which are based on mineral or glass fibre, and are generally used nowadays only for outbuildings. More expensive high-performance felts based on polyester fibres and fabrics are more durable. As an alternative to bonding each felt layer to the one below with bitumen, torch-on felts have been developed. These have bitumen on one face that is melted with a blow-torch as the felt is unrolled into position.

The top layer of felt needs protecting against the effects of sunlight. Solar protection is usually provided by dressing the roof surface with a layer of small stone chippings, or by applying a solar reflective paint. Chippings are best bonded to the felt surface to prevent them from drifting into gutters, but bonded chippings are difficult to remove if the roof needs repairing.

Asphalt is a seamless roof covering made from natural or synthetic bitumen. It is melted in a cauldron and applied hot, over a layer of sheathing felt, in two layers to a total thickness of 18–20mm. It is used as an alternative to built-up felt on roofs that are used as balconies or roof gardens.

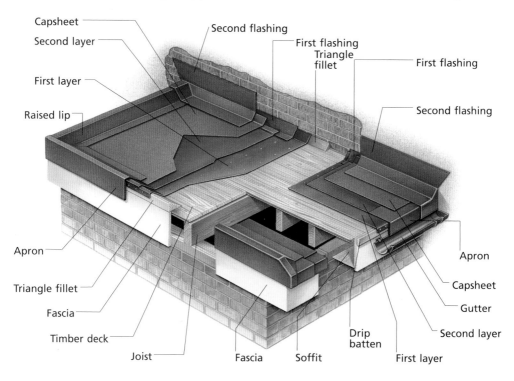

Capsheet — Second layer — First layer — Raised lip — Second flashing — First flashing — Triangle fillet — First flashing — Second flashing — Apron — Triangle fillet — Fascia — Timber deck — Joist — Fascia — Soffit — Drip batten — First layer — Second layer — Gutter — Capsheet — Apron

Insulation and ventilation

A basic flat roof is a poor insulator, with just decking above the joists and a plasterboard ceiling below to keep the heat in. Old flat roofs may contain no insulation at all, or just a thin glass fibre blanket laid above the ceiling. As a result, the rooms are cold and expensive to heat. Insulated flat roofs are divided into two categories – cold roofs and warm roofs – according to where the insulation layer is placed.

Cold roof In a cold roof, the insulation is placed above the ceiling and between the joists. The ceiling requires a vapour barrier, otherwise moisture rising through it will form condensation within the roof structure, encouraging rot. Ventilation must be provided by openings equivalent to a 25mm wide strip all round the eaves of the roof. Condensation is still a potential problem, so warm roofs are now preferred.

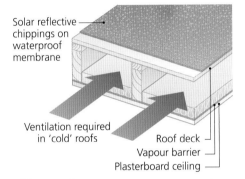

Solar reflective chippings on waterproof membrane

Ventilation required in 'cold' roofs

Roof deck
Vapour barrier
Plasterboard ceiling

Warm roof There are two main types of warm roof construction. In both, the insulation is placed above the roof deck, keeping it and the roof structure warm. This means a greatly reduced incidence of condensation, so ventilation of the roof space is no longer required, although a vapour barrier is still incorporated in the structure.

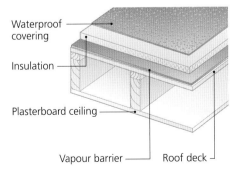

Waterproof covering

Insulation

Plasterboard ceiling

Vapour barrier   Roof deck

Sandwich roof Insulation in the form of rigid boards is placed over a vapour barrier on top of the deck, and is protected by the final roof covering.

THE TROUBLE WITH FLAT ROOFS

Failure of the roofing felt is the commonest problem with flat roofs. A standard bitumen-bonded three-layer roof has a life expectancy of 10 to 15 years if well maintained, and less if it is subjected to regular foot traffic and the careless use of ladders or other access equipment, both of which can damage the felt. Weathering of the felt opens up cracks and pinholes that allow moisture to penetrate, causing blisters in the felt when the moisture is turned to vapour in hot sun. Seams and edges can be lifted in high winds, causing the felt to tear and allowing water penetration. Once water has penetrated, dampness in the roof structure can allow rot to develop. This initially causes the decking to subside between the joists, and may eventually lead to collapse of the roof structure if not remedied.

What to do

It is important to inspect flat roofs regularly – at least once a year – so that small defects can be treated before they cause major trouble. You can repair blisters and splits yourself (see page 42) and carry out other minor repairs such as fixing faulty flashings (page 38). More widespread problems may need an overall waterproofing treatment (page 43). Full-scale replacement of an existing felted roof is a major project which you may prefer to leave to a professional.

Inverted roof The insulation is placed above the roof covering, and is held down by ballast in the form of paving stones or a layer of pebbles. This protects the roof covering from extremes of temperature and accidental damage, and can be used to upgrade the insulation of an existing roof without any structural work. It has two drawbacks. Firstly, repairs to the roof, if needed, are more difficult to carry out because the ballast and insulation must first be removed. Secondly, the ballast may impose too great a load on an insubstantial roof structure; a surveyor should always check this aspect before an inverted roof is used on an existing roof structure.

Minor repairs to flat roofs

Small blisters or cracks are the most common minor defects in felt-covered flat roofs.

Before you start Scrape off any chippings carefully with an old wallpaper scraper. You can repair small blisters or cracks with a roof-and-gutter sealant (below), with self-adhesive flashing strip (see Making a temporary repair to a cracked tile or slate, page 30), or with brush-on liquid rubber (right). Repair damaged flashings as described on page 38.

Curing bubbles A bubble may form in the felt where moisture has seeped under it and swollen in the heat of the sun. Cut a cross in the blister with a sharp knife and fold back the four flaps of felt.

Let them dry, then stick them down with a cold felt adhesive before patching the damaged area with a piece of self-adhesive flashing strip or a bitumen mastic repair compound.

Replace any roof chippings when the repairs are complete.

Bituminous sealant Apply sealant from an applicator gun to mend small cracks in roofing felt and roof tiles.

Repairing a cracked flashing

Changes in temperature and normal house movement put the flashings under stress and may cause cracks where water can seep in. The resulting wet patch indoors, however, can be several feet away from the crack because the water may run along the roof beams before dripping onto the ceiling. The crack may be difficult to spot. When you have located it, repair it with self-adhesive flashing strip (see Making repairs with flashing strip, page 38).

Repairing a hole or crack with liquid rubber

If cracks develop on a flat roof that is covered with felt or asphalt, treat the whole area with brush-on liquid rubber.

Calculate the area of the roof in square metres and buy the amount of liquid rubber recommended by the manufacturer. Liquid rubber is sold in containers ranging from 1kg to 20kg.

Tools *Ladder; stiff brush and shovel; an old 100mm paintbrush or a small broom for the liquid rubber. Perhaps a paintbrush for primer.*

Materials *Liquid rubber. Perhaps primer for liquid rubber.*

1 Use the stiff brush and shovel to clear the area of loose chippings and dirt.

2 If the area has previously been treated with a tar-bitumen coating – which gives a black, slightly rough covering – brush on a coat of primer for liquid rubber. Leave it to dry overnight.

3 Brush on a coat of liquid rubber, using all the recommended amount for the area. Leave it to dry thoroughly for 48 hours. After an hour it will be sufficiently dry not to be affected by rain.

4 Brush on a second coat of rubber, using the same amount as before.

A replacement flashing

If the flashing has cracked or corroded so much that an adhesive patch may not be able to make firm contact all over the damaged area, strip away all the flashing and plan to replace it with self-adhesive flashing strip as described in Replacing a flashing (page 39).

Seal the joint between roof and parapet (or house wall) with roof-and-gutter sealant before you apply the primer.

If your parapet is only one course of brickwork or masonry high, let the second layer of flashing overlap onto the top.

Parapet roofs

Where a flat roof is the main house roof, it is usually of the parapet type. A parapet roof may also be given to an extension or to a detached garage.

Raised edges In a parapet flat roof, the walls continue above the roof level. The parapet may be only one course of brickwork or it may be several courses.

Drainage The roof usually has a slight fall towards an opening in one side with a drainage hopper outside it connected to a downpipe that carries away rainwater. The drainage hole to the hopper must be kept clear of leaves or debris that could block it.

Flashing Where the roof meets the house wall or parapet there is a triangular wooden fillet and a flashing of lead, zinc, aluminium or felt. A cracked or displaced flashing is a frequent source of trouble.

Re-covering a parapet roof with reinforced bitumen

A reinforced bitumen covering consists of a layer of open-meshed reinforcing fabric between layers of a liquid-bitumen waterproofing solution. Both are sold by builders' merchants.

Before you start When estimating how much you will need, remember that there is no need to overlap the strips. Wear old shoes which you can throw away when you have finished, or Wellington boots which can remain dirty. When leaving the roof, change into clean shoes at the parapet, before stepping onto the ladder.

Tools *Ladder; stiff brush and shovel; filling knife; paintbrush; sharp knife; wallpaper seam roller; soft broom or large cheap paintbrush for the liquid bitumen.*

Materials *Roof-and-gutter sealant; flashing strip primer; self adhesive flashing strip; bitumen solution; reinforcing fabric, such as Aquaseal glass-fibre membrane.*

1 Brush the surface clean of any loose dirt and debris.

2 Press roof-and-gutter sealant into any cracks or holes, using a filling knife.

3 Apply a coat of flashing-strip primer to a 150mm strip at the roof edge and a similar strip of the parapet or house wall adjoining. Let it dry for 30 minutes to an hour.

4 Cut and fit lengths of flashing strip as described in Replacing a flashing (page 39). Continue the flashing round the sides of the opening for the drainage hopper and let it lap onto the surface of the brick or stonework. Fit a patch under the external angles as shown on page 39.

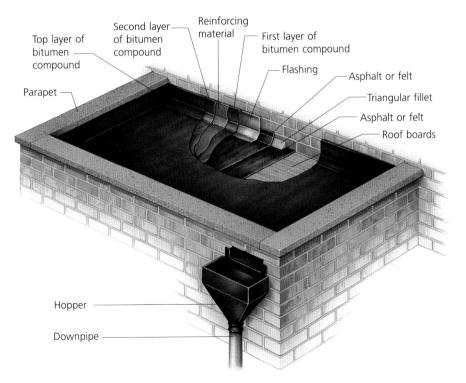

Top layer of bitumen compound — Second layer of bitumen compound — Reinforcing material — First layer of bitumen compound — Flashing — Asphalt or felt — Parapet — Triangular fillet — Asphalt or felt — Roof boards — Hopper — Downpipe

5 Cut strips of reinforcing fabric to length, allowing for them to extend 150mm up the wall at each edge. Do not lay them yet.

6 Apply a coat of liquid-bitumen waterproofing solution to the roof using a soft broom or paintbrush. The coat should be applied about 150mm up any walls that enclose the roof as well and should cover the whole flat surface and the opening to the hopper.

7 Leave for a few minutes, until the surface is tacky. Then lay the fabric strips side by side over the whole flat area and to the top of the tacky rim round all the walls. At the corners of the parapet fold the excess fabric into a neat pleat and press it flat.

8 Brush a second coat of the liquid bitumen waterproofing solution over the whole area. Apply the solution generously, especially at the parapet corners, so that you avoid dislodging the reinforcing fabric as much as possible. Then leave the surface to dry.

HIGH-LEVEL SAFETY

No matter how small the task, any DIY work done on a roof carries an element of danger.
• If you are working on a roof, make sure the ladder you use is securely supported. If possible have a helper with you to keep the ladder steady; if this is impossible, secure the ladder to the roof or to the building.
• Never lean over to reach a patch of roof – move the ladder instead.

---

9 After about two hours brush a final coat of the liquid bitumen waterproofing solution all over the flat area and 150mm up the enclosing walls.

Mending a corrugated plastic roof

A corrugated plastic roof is ideal where extra light is required, but it can become brittle and need repairing.

Before you start Measure the profile of the existing plastic on the roof before you go to buy new sheeting. The sheets may have a round or a box profile and the difference between the lowest and highest points of the profile can vary from 38 to 150mm.

If the new plastic does not exactly match the old in profile, it will not make snug overlaps. The length of the screws you use must be the difference between the low and high points of the profile plus at least 25mm to penetrate the wood.

To reduce the cost of the repair, you can fit a patch. However, the patch will have to be the width of a full sheet and extend over a roof timber at top and bottom to be screwed in place.

Temporary repairs to a corrugated plastic roof can be made using clear waterproof tape. Ensure surfaces are clean and dry before pressing the tape into place.

Tools *Sharp knife; tack lifter; screwdriver; fine-toothed saw; hand drill with blunt twist bit, or electric soldering iron with 5mm bit; steel measuring tape.*

Materials *Enough corrugated plastic sheeting to make the repair with adequate overlaps; No. 8 galvanised screws of appropriate length; protective screw caps; transparent waterproof glazing tape.*

Fitting a patch

1 Use a felt pen to mark cutting lines on the damaged panel showing the area for removal. Make the top line just below a timber support and the bottom line just above a timber support.

2 Prise off the screw caps with the tack lifter and take out all the screws that were securing the panel. Carefully remove the whole panel.

3 Cut the patch to overlap the guidelines on the old panel by 75mm at top and bottom. Then cut along the guidelines on the old panel to remove the damaged part. Hold the saw at a shallow angle and support the sheet on both sides of the cut. If you have to cut to the sheet to width, cut along the valleys of the sheeting.

4 Lay the plastic for the bottom of the slope in place first. Make screw holes through the peaks that are over timbers. Make the holes at intervals of about 450mm across the panel immediately above the cross timbers. You can melt the holes with a fine soldering iron, start them with a bradawl, or use a blunt bit in a drill. Drive in the screws across the bottom edge. Do not overtighten.

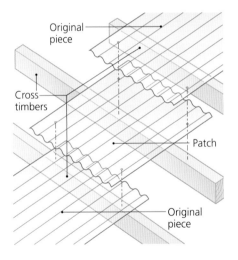

Original piece

Cross timbers

Patch

Original piece

5 Lay the next piece of plastic up the slope; let its bottom edge overlap 75mm onto the piece below.

6 Drill screw holes through peaks on the overlap at 450mm intervals. Drive screws through into the timbers but do not overtighten them.

7 Lay the top piece of plastic in place overlapping the previous piece by 75mm.

8 Drill and screw the bottom edge as for the previous piece.

9 Drill holes if necessary at the top edge and screw it in place.

10 Push caps on all the screws.

11 Fit new flashing strip (page 39) where the plastic sheet meets the wall. Press it down well into the valleys.

12 Seal the edges where the layers of plastic sheeting overlap at the sides with strips of the glazing tape.

Fitting a whole panel

1 Cut away any flashing at the top of the damaged panel.

2 Prise off the screw caps with the tack lifter and take out all the screws that were securing the panel, then remove the panel.

3 Cut the new panel if necessary to match the length of the old one. Keep the saw at a shallow angle and take care to support the sheet on both sides of the cut.

4 Place the new panel in position on the roof, overlapping onto the old ones at either side. If there is another panel above or below the new one, make sure that the bottom edge of the panel higher up the slope laps onto the panel below.

5 Make screw holes across the bottom if necessary at 450mm intervals immediately above the cross timbers. Melt the holes with a fine soldering iron, start them with a bradawl, or a blunt bit in a drill.

6 Drive in the screws; do not over tighten them or the plastic may split.

7 When the screws are fixed, push on screw caps. Follow steps 11 and 12 as in 'Fitting a patch'.

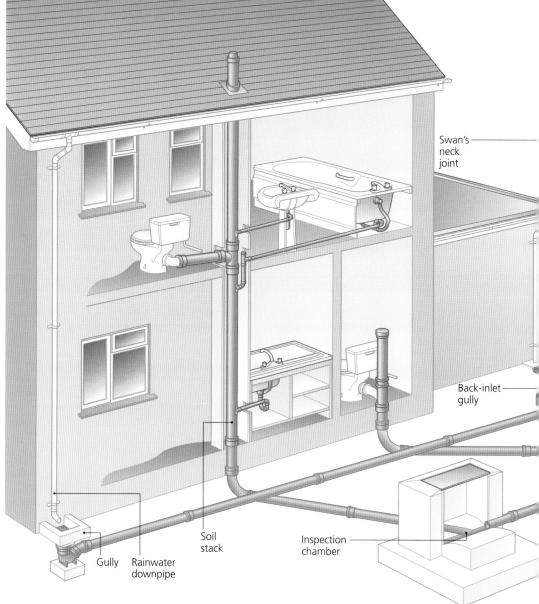

Swan's
neck
joint

Back-inlet
gully

Soil
stack

Inspection
chamber

Gully   Rainwater
downpipe

Rainwater and drainage systems

Neglected leaks and blockages can lead to damp, unsightly stains and floods. Make sure that all gutters, pipes and drains flow freely.

Water running off a roof is collected in gutters fixed to the fascia boards. The gutters must be big enough to collect the occasional downpour without overflowing, and for most houses a gutter 100 or 112mm in width will do the job.

They discharge the water they collect into downpipes, which run down the house walls to ground level and empty the water into gullies. A downpipe 68–75mm in diameter is usually big enough to carry the discharge from 100 or 112mm gutters.

Gutter outlets These are fitted at downpipe positions, discharging directly into the downpipe if the house eaves are flush with the wall. If the eaves overhang, an offset double-bend pipe called a swan's neck links the gutter to the downpipe.

Where two roof slopes meet in a valley, the rainwater is usually discharged from the valley gutter into a fitting called a hopper. A downpipe runs from the hopper down to ground level. A rainwater hopper may also collect waste water from upstairs baths and washbasins.

Cast iron downpipes Iron pipes have integral fixing lugs that are secured to the house walls with large pipe nails driven into wooden wedges in the mortar joints of the wall. Each pipe end fits loosely into the top of the length below. Bends divert the pipe where necessary, and single branch fittings allow two downpipes to be joined. At the base of the pipe, an angled fitting called a shoe discharges the water over the grate of an underground gully.

uPVC rainwater systems In most modern houses, gutter systems are plastic. They are very similar to their cast iron counterparts in terms of the components used, but are much lighter. They are available in black, grey, white and brown.

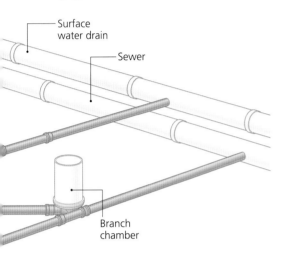

Surface
water drain

Sewer

Branch
chamber

Joints are made using fittings with integral rubber seals and plastic clips. The gutters may be half-round, or may have a deep oval or square trough cross-section. All are supported on brackets screwed to the fascia boards. The gutters discharge into downpipes that are fixed to the wall with separate brackets.

Aluminium gutters These are seamless, and are formed on site by passing lengths of aluminium strip through a shaping machine. The lengths are joined to special outlet, angle and stop-end fittings to make up the gutter run. Matching downpipes are available to complete the system.

Gullies

At ground level, downpipes discharge into an underground fitting called a gully. If rainwater and waste water flow into the same drains, the gully contains a U-bend which prevents drain smells from rising up the downpipes. The bend also acts as a trap for debris washed down from the roof slope, preventing it from being washed into the drains.

• In old houses, the gullies will be made of earthenware (called vitrified clay), also used for the underground drains (below). Modern houses have plastic (uPVC) gullies and drains.
• If the house has separate rainwater and waste water drains, a trap is not needed and the downpipes can be connected directly to the underground rainwater drain by an underground elbow fitting. The gully may be a single round or square pot, with the downpipe shoe discharging over it through a grating that can be removed for cleaning if the trap becomes blocked.
• If the gully also drains water from a garden, it may have two inlets – one for the downpipe and another to take surface water. This type is a back-inlet gully.
• In modern plastic installations, the downpipe does not discharge over a grating, but passes through it, straight into the gully trap. A removable grating allows access to the trap for cleaning.
• If the house has separate rainwater drains, the downpipe is connected to the drains via an underground elbow, with a ground-level access point nearby to allow blockages to be cleared if they occur.

THE TROUBLE WITH GUTTERS AND DRAINS

By far the most common problem with both rainwater and drainage systems is a blockage, leading to an overflow from the affected part of the system. This may be caused by leaves and wind-blown debris in gutters and hoppers, or by unsuitable materials being flushed into the drainage system.

Leaks are another problem. They are easily solved in rainwater systems but more difficult to tackle in underground drains.

Old cast iron gutters often suffer from serious (and sometimes terminal) rust.

What to do
Clearing blockages, fixing leaks and dealing with other rainwater system problems is generally a simple matter of routine maintenance (see pages 49–55) You can tackle most drain blockages yourself with the aid of a set of drain rods, which you can buy or hire when required (see pages 53–55).

Underground drains

Drains are a mysterious underworld to most homeowners, and are noticed only if they get blocked. Knowing where they run and how they work makes dealing with this occasional occurrence much less traumatic.

Soil stacks Homes built since about the 1950s have one or more uPVC soil stacks to gather all the household waste water and carry it into the drains. All appliances – including WCs – are connected directly into the stack, which is sited inside the house to do away with all the unsightly external plumbing of the old two-pipe system.

Manholes Each stack discharges into a manhole, which may be a traditional rectangular brick chamber or a plastic moulding fitted with a round metal cover. Extra manholes are installed to connect in other branch drains, or at any point where the drain run changes direction. Finally the drain run connects into the main sewer.

Soakaways Rainwater is collected separately from waste water, and is taken by buried pipes to a main surface water drain or into a sunken chamber called a soakaway. They are usually buried in both front and rear gardens, and allow the collected rainwater to soak away into the subsoil.

Cesspools and septic tanks

In areas where there is no mains drainage system, household waste water can be led into an underground cesspool – a large holding tank that has to be emptied regularly for disposal elsewhere.

A septic tank is a tiny sewage treatment plant, breaking down the material piped into it by a combination of filtration and bacterial action. The effluent is safe enough to be discharged into the subsoil, and residual solid material has to be cleaned out of the tank from time to time.

OLDER HOMES

In houses built before about 1950, a two-pipe system carried waste water from the house (and often rainwater from the roof as well) to the underground drains. One large-diameter pipe called the soil pipe took waste from WCs directly into the drains by an underground elbow; a trap to keep drain smells out was not needed because the WC pan contained one, but the pipe was extended to eaves level to ventilate the drain section.

Waste water discharged directly into a trapped gully from appliances such as a sink at ground-floor level, or into a wall-mounted hopper from basins and other appliances in upstairs rooms.

A downpipe linked the hopper to the gully below, which was connected to a separate section of the drains. All these pipes were mounted on the walls of the house, and looked extremely unsightly.

The underground section of the soil pipe and the drain run from each gully met at an underground brick chamber called an inspection chamber or manhole, fitted with a cast iron cover. Inside the manhole, the branch pipes run into an open channel, allowing each section of the drains to be cleared via the manhole using drain rods if it became blocked. The outlet from the chamber ran on as a single underground drain, via further manholes installed to connect in other branch drains or where the drain run changed direction. The last manhole before the main sewer was built as an interceptor manhole, and contained a trap to prevent sewer gases from entering the drainage system of individual houses. This type of manhole was prone to frequent blockages, and has not been used for many years.

Hopper
Gully

Repairing leaking gutter joints

Sometimes you can spot a dripping gutter from indoors, but it is best to check your gutters from the outside during a heavy downpour.

Rainwater dripping through gutters and splashing the house walls will cause a water stain on the outside wall and, after a time, moss and algae will grow, disfiguring the wall. If the leak is not cured, damp will penetrate the walls, causing damage indoors. Damp quickly ruins decorations and eventually causes rot in timbers.

Leaking metal gutters

A metal gutter is difficult to take apart if the nuts and bolts have corroded, so try to seal the leak by injecting roof-and-gutter sealant into the joint with an applicator gun. First scrape the joint clean and dry it with a hot-air gun. If the leak persists, you will have to dismantle and reseal the joint. Wear strong gloves to protect your hands from rough metal.

Tools *Ladder with a stand-off bracket; gloves; safety goggles; spanner; hammer; wire brush; old chisel; small trowel; paintbrush; narrow-bladed filing knife. Perhaps a junior hacksaw and nail punch.*

Materials *Metal primer; roof-and-gutter sealant; nut and bolt of correct size.*

1 Undo the nut securing the bolt in the joint piece.

Alternatively If the nut will not move, cut through the bolt with a hacksaw and take out the shank with nail punch and hammer.

2 Gently hammer the joint piece to separate it from the gutter sections.

3 With the joint dismantled, chisel away the putty and clean rust from the whole joint area with the wire brush. Scoop away the debris with the trowel.

4 Apply a coat of metal primer to the gutter ends and the joint piece and leave it to dry.

5 Spread roof-and-gutter sealant onto the joint piece and reposition the gutter sections on it.

6 Secure the joint with the new nut and bolt.

Leaking plastic gutters

Where pieces of gutter join, or connect with a downpipe, they are clipped to a connector or union piece which has gaskets in it to make the union watertight.
    Leakages caused by dirt forcing the seal slightly apart can be cured by cleaning. Squeeze the sides of the gutter inwards to release it from the union piece. If there is no dirt, the gaskets may need renewing.

Tools *Ladder with a stand-off bracket; filling knife.*

Materials *New gaskets or roof-and-gutter sealant.*

1 Squeeze the sides of the gutter sections in order to release them from the clips of the union piece.

2 Gently raise the end of each section of gutter in turn until you can see the gasket in the union piece. Peel the gasket away.

3 Fit the new gaskets, pressing them well into place.

4 Gently squeeze each gutter section in at the sides to ease it back into the union piece clips.

Re-aligning a gutter

If water forms a pool, even in a cleaned gutter, instead of running away to the downpipe, the fixing screw holding the support bracket or the gutter itself at that point may be loose.

Remove the screw, tap a wall plug into the screw hole and re-screw the bracket or gutter with a new zinc-plated screw. If, when you check, you find that no screws are loose, or conversely that several are loose, the fall of the gutter may need correcting. You may have to remove a section of gutter to reach the screws.

Tools *Ladder with a stand-off bracket; hammer; screwdriver; drill with wood bit or high-speed-steel bit, or both.*

Materials *Wall plugs; zinc-plated No. 8 or No. 10 screws; two or more 150mm nails; string and nails.*

1 Drive a long, strong nail into the fascia board near each end of the loose section of gutter, immediately below it, to support it. If the loose section is longer than 2m or the gutter is iron, drive in more nails to give it sufficient support.

2 Remove the screws that hold the gutter or its supporting brackets.

3 Fix a taut string line along the length of the fascia board immediately under the guttering. This will act as a guide. Give it a fall towards the downpipe of 15–20mm in every 3m.

4 If the gutter is on brackets, unscrew those that are letting the gutter sag and move them left or right to new positions so that you can screw into solid wood; make sure the new screw positions align with the string line to give the correct fall.

Alternatively If the gutter is screwed direct to the fascia, raise it to align correctly with the string line and drill new holes through the gutter and into the fascia, about 50mm to the side of the original holes. Refit the gutter using new zinc-plated screws.

Alternatively If the screws through the gutter have been driven into the ends of the roof rafters, fix a string line and adjust the position of the screws to bring the gutter to the correct fall. You may have to remove a tile or slate temporarily so that you can reach the screws.

Cleaning an overflowing gutter

Gutters should be cleaned out and checked for damage each year. The job is best done in late autumn after all the leaves have fallen.

Before you start Wear sturdy work gloves to avoid scraping your hands on rough or rusty edges or on tiles or slates.

Tools *Ladder with a stand-off bracket; small trowel; bucket; piece of hardboard or a large rag. Possibly a hosepipe.*

1 Put the piece of hardboard at the bottom of the downpipe to prevent debris from getting into the gully or the drain, where it could cause a blockage.

Alternatively If the downpipe goes direct into the ground, stuff the rag in the top of it.

2 Scoop out any silt, grit or other debris with the trowel and put it into the bucket. Take care not to let anything drop into the downpipe. Take care not to let any debris fall down the walls because it may cause stains that are hard to remove.

3 Unblock the downpipe and pour three or four buckets of water slowly into the gutter at the end farthest from the pipe.

Alternatively Use a hosepipe to lead water there. The water should flow quickly and smoothly to the downpipe, leaving the gutter empty.
• If a pool of water remains, the gutter needs realigning.
• If the water leaks through cracks or bad joints, repair the gutter (page 49).
• If the water starts to overflow at the downpipe, the pipe needs cleaning out.

Securing loose downpipes

A downpipe is held to the wall by retaining clips that are screwed into the mortar joints at intervals of about a metre.

If the pipe is not firmly held, it vibrates in strong winds, and this can loosen its joints. The sections of downpipe slot loosely one into another; do not seal them together.

Cast-iron pipes

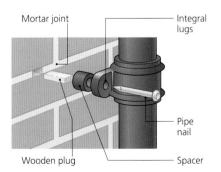

Mortar joint — Integral lugs — Pipe nail — Wooden plug — Spacer

The lugs that hold cast-iron pipes are an integral part of the pipe and are fixed with large nails called pipe nails to wooden plugs

inserted in the mortar joints. If only the nails are loose, take them out and fill the hole with wood filler or insert a wall plug into it. Drive the pipe nails back in, or drive in 38mm No. 10 galvanised screws instead.

If the wooden plugs in the wall have come loose or rotted; you will have to remove them and fix new ones.

Plastic downpipes

If a plastic downpipe comes loose from the wall, check the screws and the plastic or fibre wall plugs to see if they need renewing to give a better fixing. Use 38mm No. 10 galvanised screws.

It might be easier to move the clip up or down a little to a different mortar joint, and drill and plug new holes to get a firm fixing. Repair the old holes with mortar or exterior filler. Match the colour of the rest of the mortar to make the repair discreet.

Do not move a clip fixed at a joint in the downpipe system because it strengthens the joint. You could exchange a one-piece clip for a two-piece clip, or vice-versa, to give different fixing positions for screws.

Unblocking a downpipe

Overflow from a gutter may be caused by a blocked downpipe.

Before you start Check what is causing the blockage. It could be a ball, a bird's nest or some other object that you can simply lift out. But the most likely obstruction is a collection of wind-blown leaves lodged in the mouth of the downpipe.

A pipe with a swan-necked section at the top is more likely to become blocked than a straight downpipe.

Another indication of a blocked down-pipe is water seeping out during heavy rain from a joint where sections of downpipe connect. Because the joints are loose, not sealed, you can tell straight away where the blockage is; it is in the section immediately below the leaking joint.

Obstructions near the top

If the downpipe is blocked near the top, you can usually clear it by probing with a length of wire. Cover the drain at the bottom of the pipe to prevent any debris from falling into it. Hook out debris if you can; if you cannot, probe until it becomes loose. Flush away remaining loose debris by pouring buckets of water down the pipe or playing a strong jet of water down it from a hose. If the pipe is straight, not swan-necked, tie rags firmly to the end of a stick (such as a bamboo garden cane) to form a ball and push the obstruction loose with it.

Obstructions out of reach

Hire a flexible drain rod to clear an obstruction lower down a pipe or in a swan-necked pipe. Or, as a last resort, dismantle the lower part of the downpipe.

Tools *Ladder with a stand-off bracket; screwdriver or pliers or box spanner; long stick. Perhaps a cold chisel and claw hammer.*

---

1 On a plastic downpipe, remove the screws that hold the pipe clips to the wall. Work from the bottom and remove the screws and clips up to the point it leaks. If the pipe is held by two-part brackets, undo the bolts holding the rings to the back plates; leave the back plates in place.
 If the pipe is cast-iron, use pliers to pull out the large pipe nails that hold the lugs to the wall. If they are rusted, use a cold chisel and claw hammer to prise the lugs from the wall; keep the nails for re-use.

2 As you free the clips or lugs that hold it, free each section of pipe from the section below and lift it away from the wall.

3 Use a long stick to push out any obstructions inside the sections.

4 Replace the pipe section by section, working from the top down, and screw or bolt back in place the clips (or nail the lugs) that hold the section to the wall.

Preventing blockages

Wire or plastic covers are sold in different sizes for fitting in mouths of downpipes.
• If there is a hopper at the top of the downpipe, fit fine-mesh wire netting over the top, securing it with fine galvanised wire.
• If there are large deciduous trees nearby, it is worth covering gutters. Lay a strip of plastic netting over a gutter to overlap the top by about 50mm at each side. About every 1m along it, thread a length of twine

through the overlaps from the underside of the gutter and tie it firmly to hold the mesh taut. Check the netting surface regularly during autumn; if leaves coat it, rain cannot enter the gutter and will spill over it.

Cleaning and maintaining gullies

A gully is an underground U-trap that prevents bulky waste from flowing into the drains. It is prone to blockage.

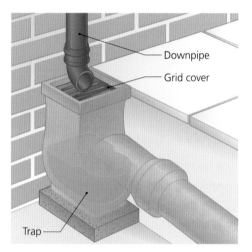

Downpipe

Grid cover

Trap

A gully is fitted at the point where a downpipe or waste pipe discharges at ground level, and is then connected to the underground drains. A yard gully is similar, but is sited away from the house and collects surface water via an open grating. The trap in the gully is there to collect solid waste material, preventing it from entering the drains and causing a blockage that would be difficult to remove.
 In older properties, the water discharges into a gully above a grid fitted over the trap. This grid can become blocked with leaves and other debris, resulting in waste water splashing over the surrounding area instead of passing into the trap.
 In newer properties, waste pipes discharge into soil stacks, and downpipes discharge into back-inlet gullies. Here the downpipe passes directly through the grating and into the trap, so avoiding over-flow problems. If the gully does not have to act as a yard gully, a screw-down cover provides access to the trap.

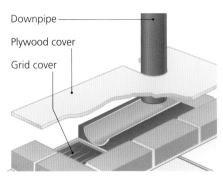

Downpipe

Plywood cover

Grid cover

Channel gullies taking waste water via a half-round channel are especially prone to grid blockages. Prevent these by putting a cover on the gully. Cut it from outdoor-grade plywood 13–19mm thick. Make a hole for the waste pipe to pass through.

Clearing a blockage

1 Clear all debris from the gully grating. If necessary, prise out the grating and scrub it in hot soapy water.

2 If the blockage is deeper, remove the grating. Wear long rubber gloves or put your arm in a plastic bag. Reach into the trap, which may be up to 600mm deep, and scoop out as much debris as you can.

3 If the obstruction is too solid to scoop out, break it down with a garden trowel.

4 When the gully is cleared, scrub the sides with a nylon pot scourer and hose them down with a fierce jet of water. Disinfect all gloves and tools afterwards.

5 If you cannot find an obstruction in the gully, the blockage may be farther down the drain (see Clearing blocked drains, page 54).

Repairing a channel gully

A channel sometimes runs parallel with the house wall to lead water into a gully entrance or to hold water that comes too fast for the gully to take. The channel can crack or become loose. The rendering around it can also crack or develop hollows where water lodges and stagnates.

Repair damaged rendering with a mix of one part cement to four parts soft sand, with PVA building adhesive added for a better bond. Alternatively, buy a small bag of dry-mix sand-cement mortar to use instead, but add PVA adhesive to improve adhesion. Give the repair a smooth finish so that water does not collect.

Renewing a damaged gully

You will have to chip out the old one and the surrounding brick and rendering. You can buy ready-made vitrified clay channels from builders' merchants. Use the same mortar mix as for rendering repairs.

Tools *Chalk; cold chisel; club hammer; offcut of hardboard or thick card; trowel.*

Materials *Bricks; length of channel; mortar.*

1 To cut the channel to length, first measure and mark the length at several points round the pipe and join the marks with a chalk line. Lay the channel on a heap of sand and use the chisel and hammer to chip round the marked line until the channel breaks along it. Alternatively, use an angle grinder if you have one to cut the channel. Wear goggles to protect your eyes from flying dust and chippings.

2 Put a piece of hardboard over the gully inlet to prevent debris from getting in.

3 Chip out the damaged channel and the mortar and any bricks round it. If the bricks round the gully entrance are damaged, chip these out as well. Brush up the debris.

4 Mix the mortar and spread a thick layer where the channel will lie. Bed down the channel on it, setting it so that it slopes slightly towards the gully.

5 Lay a course of bricks on edge to make a low retaining wall round the channel and gully. Set them on a bed of mortar and leave a gap of at least 25mm between the channel and the bricks alongside it. Nearer the gully the gap may need to be wider.

6 Fill the gap between the channel and the bricks with mortar.

7 Slope the mortar smoothly up to the brick surround and make sure there are no hollows to trap water.

Clearing blocked drains

Below ground, pipes carry water and waste from the house to the main drain outside the boundary of the property, or to a cesspool or septic tank. Rainwater may be led separately into the drain or into a soakaway.

Before you start Remember that the pipes below ground are laid in straight lines for as much of their route as possible. Where a change of direction is needed, the bend should be less than a right angle and there should be an inspection chamber there. A manhole cover identifies the chambers. An older property may have an interceptor chamber near the boundary before the house drain joins the main drain (see right).

The first sign of a blocked drain may be the failure of WCs and baths to drain quickly and efficiently, or an overflowing inspection chamber or gully. A gully may be cleared by cleaning (page 52). Otherwise you will have to clear the drain with rods. You can hire rods and various heads. Wear rubber gloves for the work.

Tools *Drain rods fitted with a 100mm diameter rubber plunger; pair of long rubber gloves; strong garden spade; hose; disinfectant; watering can.*

1 Locate the blockage. You will have to lift the manhole covers; a strong garden spade will raise the edge enough for you to grasp the cover. Inspect the chamber that is nearer to the main drain, septic tank or cesspool than the overflowing chamber or gully. If it is empty, the blockage is in the drain between this chamber and the higher one or the gully. If the chamber is full, inspect the chamber next nearest to the main drain or septic tank. If the chamber nearest the main drain is full, the blockage is between it and the main drain. If the drain leads to a septic tank and the last chamber is full, have the tank emptied.

2 To clear the blockage in a main drain system, insert the rod fitted with the plunger into a chamber at one end of the blocked section; it does not matter which of the two. If it is the empty chamber, you can see where the mouth of the pipe is, but if you work from the full chamber, you will have to probe with the plunger until you find the mouth.

3 Add more rods as necessary to work the plunger along the pipe to the blockage. Always turn the rods clockwise as you work; if you turn them counter-clockwise, they may unscrew and be left in the drain to cause a greater problem. Keep pushing against the obstruction and then withdrawing the plunger a little way.

If this will not shift the blockage, withdraw the rods and exchange the plunger for a corkscrew attachment, which will break up a tightly packed obstruction.

4 Complete the clearance by directing a strong jet of water down the drain from a hosepipe, or by filling the bath and sink and releasing the water in one gush.

5 Hose down the rods and gloves thoroughly and drench them with diluted disinfectant poured from a watering can.

Testing drains

If the drains are not blocked, but a persistent foul smell or unexpectedly wet ground make you suspect that there is a leak somewhere, arrange for the environmental health department to test the drains. You can get in touch with the department at your local authority offices.

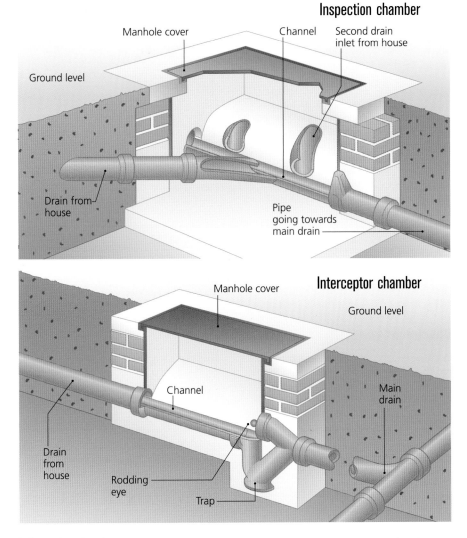

Inspection chamber

Manhole cover

Channel

Second drain inlet from house

Ground level

Drain from house

Pipe going towards main drain

Interceptor chamber

Manhole cover

Ground level

Channel

Main drain

Drain from house

Rodding eye

Trap

Interceptor chambers If you have to clear a blockage between an interceptor chamber on your property and the main drain, you will have to insert the rods through the rodding eye. At this chamber, the drain drops through a U-trap similar to the one in a gully. The trap is there to prevent waste from the main drain entering your house drains, but it also prevents you from pushing rods through. Above the mouth of the trap there is a short projection of pipe with a plug in it. When you locate and pull out the plug, you can insert the drain rods through the hole, or rodding eye.

The trap, however, may still be blocked and you will have to scoop out the blockage with an old garden trowel bent to a right angle. When the chamber and trap are clear, hose them down thoroughly to make sure waste can flow out easily. You can either replace the plug or you can mortar a piece of tile over the eye. If you need to open the rodding eye again, the tile will knock off easily with a crowbar and hammer.

Fence repair and maintenance

Don't forget to include the garden in your survey. Posts and fences need regular maintenance to last.

Timber rots in contact with earth, so whenever possible keep it from direct contact with the ground and treat fences and other garden woodwork regularly with wood preservative to prolong their life. Never pile soil against a wooden fence. Timber fence posts are most likely to rot at the bottom and below ground, and will eventually collapse and bring down part of the fence unless reinforced in good time. To prevent a post rotting from the top downwards, slope the top or fit a post cap.

Feather-edged boards often get brittle and start to crack if they are not kept well protected with preservative. So do arris rails (page 58), which take a lot of strain in supporting feather-edged boards or palings, and will quickly get worse unless repaired.

Reinforcing a fence post

If the main part of a rotting post is still sound, it can be supported with a concrete spur or it can be cut short and refitted with its base in a metal post spike. If the rot extends higher than the top of the gravel board (page 59), you will have to free the fencing from the post before you can cut the rot out. It may be simpler to replace the post.

Tools *Handsaw; old paintbrush; timber lengths for fence supports; timber length for compacting concrete; spade; hammer; drill and 13mm auger bit; spirit level; spanner; hacksaw.*

Materials *Wood preservative (page 59); concrete spur; two 10mm diameter coach bolts about 200mm long; nut and washer for each bolt; concrete foundation mix.*

1 Temporarily support the fence on each side of the post with pieces of timber.

2 Remove the gravel board and cut the rotten post back to sound wood.

3 Coat the whole post, especially the bottom and end grain, with wood preservative.

4 Dig out a hole alongside the damaged post to a depth of about 450–600mm. Make the hole at least 300mm square.

5 Put the spur in the hole, fitted snugly against the post.

6 Slip coach bolts through the holes in the spur and strike them firmly with a hammer to mark their positions on the post.

7 Remove the spur and bore holes through the post at the marked spot.

8 Push the bolts through the post and spur so that the tails are on the spur side. Slip on the washers and nuts and tighten the nuts with a spanner.

9 Use a spirit level to check that the post is vertical, pushing it upright as necessary. Then brace it firmly with lengths of timber.

10 Ram hardcore into the bottom of the spur hole, then pour in the mixed concrete, pressing it well down with the end of a piece of timber.

11 Wait 24 hours before moving the timber supports, to give the concrete time to set. Use a hacksaw to cut off protruding bolt threads slightly proud of the nuts.

Replacing a timber fence post

Tools *Pincers or claw hammer; narrow spade; spirit level; length of timber longer than distance between posts; timber lengths for supporting post; earth rammer. Possibly also timber length; nails; strong rope; pile of about five or six bricks.*

Materials *Treated fence post the same size as the old one; hardcore – probably 3–6 bucketfuls; two or three arris-rail brackets (see page 58); 50mm galvanised nails.*

1 Support the fence on each side of the post with lengths of timber, wedged under the panel top or upper arris rail.

2 Free the post from the fencing. Undo panels by removing the nails or clips on each side. For vertical closeboard fencing, remove the first board on one side and saw through the arris rails. Remove nails holding the rails to the other side of the post so that they can be pulled out when the post is moved.

3 Dig down beside the post to free it at the bottom. Then remove the post and clear the hole. Replace the hardcore in the bottom of the hole to a depth of 150mm, well rammed down.

4 Insert the new post between the fence panels. On a closeboard fence, fit the shaped arris rails on one side into the slots as you put the post in. Lay a length of timber across to the next post and use a spirit level to check that the tops are level.

5 Make sure the fencing will fit flush on both sides and use a spirit level to check that the post is vertical. Fill the hole with

layers of hardcore and a mixture of soil and gravel or concrete, ramming the surface well down. Slope the top layer of concrete so that rainwater runs away from the post.

Alternatively Drive in a metal post spike using a sledgehammer and a driving tool, or dolly. Stop at regular intervals and use a spirit level to check that the spike is vertical, otherwise the post will be out of true when fitted. Use the handles of the driving tool to twist or level the spike as necessary. Continue driving until the bottom of the cup is level with the ground surface then fit the post into the cup.

6 Refit sawn off arris rails using metal brackets (page 58). Refit panels with nails or clips. If the post top is square cut, either cut it to a slope or fit a cap (see below). Treat sawn areas with wood preservative.

Repairing a post top

Saw off a rotten post back to sound wood. Timber or metal caps are sold ready to use. Soak a home-made wooden cap in wood preservative for 24 hours before fitting. The cap should be 15mm wider than the post all round. Nail it in place with two ring nails driven in at an angle from each side. A metal post cap can be made from a sheet of zinc or aluminium cut about 25mm wider than the post top and turned down round the edges.

Mending a cracked arris rail

Strengthen a rail cracked in the middle with a straight arris-rail bracket – a metal bracket about 300mm long, shaped to fit the rail, with ready-made holes for screws or nails. Fasten it with galvanised or alloy 25mm screws or 50mm nails.

If the crack is near a post, use a flanged arris-rail bracket. The two flanges – projecting lugs at right angles to the bracket – are fastened to the post. If the post is concrete, use screws and wall plugs to fasten the flange to the post.

Tighten a loose arris rail by pinning it with a 10mm grooved hardwood dowel about 50mm long. Drill a hole for the dowel through the front of the post about 20mm from the edge where the loose rail fits. Before inserting the dowel, coat it all over with waterproof adhesive. The grooves release excess glue and trapped air.

Replacing a broken arris rail

If the fence posts are concrete, the rails may be bolted to recesses in them, and are easy to replace. Or they may be fitted into mortises in the same way as timber posts, and can be repaired as described here.

Tools *Panel saw; hammer; plane or shaping tool; pencil.*

Materials *Arris rail, normally 2.4m long, treated with wood preservative; flanged arris-rail bracket (see left); 50mm galvanised or alloy nails.*

1 Hammer the boards or palings away from the damaged rail.

2 Withdraw the nails if possible and pull the damaged rail from the slots at each end. Otherwise, saw through the rail flush with the post at one end.

3 Shape one end of the new rail to fit into the post slot. Fit the new rail into the slot, mark where it will fit flush against the post at the other end and saw it to length.

4 Refit the rail into the slot, and fix the other end to the post using the flanged bracket. Refit the boards or pales to the rail, making sure they are vertical.

Replacing a panel

Fence panels are made in standard sizes, so removing a damaged panel and fitting a new one in the same way is not usually difficult.

If the new panel is slightly too wide, plane off a small amount of the frame on each side. If, however, it is not wide enough, close the gap with a narrow fillet of wood inserted between the post and the panel frame. Remember to treat the wood fillet with preservative before fixing it.

Replacing a gravel board

If for any reason a rotting gravel board cannot be replaced without dismantling the fence – if it slots into concrete posts, for example – nail the new board to timber battens fitted beside the posts.

Remove the damaged board by drilling and sawing through flush with the posts at each end. For a closeboard fence, remove a fence board at each end to make room for sawing. Support a panel on bricks (above).

Treat the new gravel board and the timber battens with wood preservative at least 24 hours before fitting them.

For timber posts, use 150mm battens, which can be nailed to the posts. For concrete posts use battens 600mm long, drive about 450mm into the ground beside the posts, as near as any concrete bedding will allow.

Dig a shallow groove under the fence to make way for the new board. Fix the battens so that the board can be fitted flush with the front of a closeboard fence, or centrally under a panel fence. Support the battens from behind while you nail the gravel boards to them. Keep soil away from the board as much as possible.

Repairing feather-edged boarding

Replace damaged or rotten boards with new boards that have been treated with wood preservative. One nail secures two overlapped boards, so to remove a board you will have to loosen the overlapping boards as well and pull out the common nail. Undamaged boards sometimes become loose because their nails have rusted. Refit the boards using 50mm galvanised or alloy nails that will not rust.

If feather-edged boards are rotting at the bottom where there is no gravel board, saw them off along the base to leave a gap of at least 150mm. Cut and fit a gravel board.

APPLYING WOOD PRESERVATIVE

Coat existing timber fences with wood preservative regularly, particularly any joints or end grain.

Choices

A wide range of wood preservatives is available. One of the best known is creosote, which is made from tar oil. It is cheap but needs yearly application, and its fumes are unpleasant. When wet it is harmful to plants (though it is harmless when dry), and wood treated with it cannot be painted.

Most modern preservatives are either solvent-based or water-based, and contain chemicals or salts that destroy fungi and insects. Solvent-based types give off flammable fumes, and naked flames should be kept away until the preservative is quite dry – until at least 12 hours after application. Water-based types have no smell. Neither type is harmful to plants once dry, but guard against splashing any on plants while you are painting.

Application

The period between treatments depends on the type of product used and how exposed the fence is. Most modern preservatives will last 2 or 3 years. Even if timber for a new fence has been pre-treated, coat it with more preservative before you fix it in place and thoroughly soak cut ends.

The best time to apply preservative is when the wood is thoroughly dry but the sun not too hot – probably in late summer after a dry spell, with no rain expected for a day or two. Damp wood will not absorb the preservative well.

Apply preservative with an old paintbrush or a garden pressure spray. Or there are kits on the market which pump the liquid from the container to a brush.

Always follow any safety precautions given on the container. With some preservatives you should protect your skin and eyes while you are applying them.

Treated wood can then be painted the colour of your choice. Many brands contain colour and protection in one product.

Looking after a gate

Make sure you create a good first impression for visitors and potential purchasers with a gate that swings freely and is in good condition.

Keep gates well treated with timber preservative or paint to prevent rotting or rusting. Hinges can be smeared with oil or grease to guard against rust, but for latches, which are constantly handled, paint is preferable, unless they are galvanised or japanned metal.

Repairing rotten timber

Cut out small areas of rot on the gate back to sound wood and fill the cavity with a two-part wood-repair filler of the epoxy-resin type. This sets after about 15 minutes and can be sanded down with medium-grade abrasive paper or a power sander to a smooth finish. The repair will not be visible after repainting.

Rotting timber parts such as pales or braces can be replaced. Treat new timber with a wood preservative (page 59), using a clear coating if it is to be painted later, or buy pre-treated timber, which will last longer. A rotting or damaged gatepost should be replaced or repaired in the same way as a fence post (page 57); but do not use a post spike. Repair a rotting post top in the same way as you would a fence post top (page 57).

Dealing with rust

Keep a lookout for rust spots on metal gates or fittings, and remove them with abrasive paper. Repaint the area you have rubbed down immediately – rust can recur overnight. Remove severe rusting by scrubbing with a wire brush (wear safety goggles). Do not use a proprietary remover if you are going to repaint with a rust-inhibiting paint. Once the rust is removed, you can either repaint the area with a rust-neutralising primer followed by an undercoat and gloss coat, or use a one-coat paint such as Hammerite, which is both a rust-inhibitor and a finishing paint.

Repairing a sagging gate

The most common cause of a sagging gate is hinges that have worked loose, so check the condition of the hinges first. Replace loose hinge screws with longer, galvanised screws if possible. If not, tap wooden dowels (or fibre wall plugs) into the holes and use screws of the same size.

Alternatively, refit the hinges, moving them slightly so that the screws bite into firm wood. Replace worn or broken hinges.

If the hinges are in good condition, the timber joints of the gate may be loose. An isolated loose joint can be repaired by fixing a metal plate – tee, corner or straight – or an angle bracket to the joint. Try to force a waterproof adhesive up into the loose joint, then hold it together while you screw the bracket in place.

A very rickety gate should be either replaced or taken apart and remade. Clean away all old adhesive from the joints and reassemble using a waterproof adhesive. Reinforce mortise-and-tenon joints by drilling into the post and through the tongue of the tenon, then insert a glued dowel. After reassembling the gate, clamp it together while the adhesive dries.

A gate may sag because it has no diagonal brace, or because the brace is not strong enough (or the gate may have been hung on the wrong side). The brace should be firmly fitted between the cross rails on the back of the gate, with the top towards the latch. Lift and wedge the gate into its proper position and make sure that it is a good fit before fixing the brace with waterproof adhesive and galvanised screws.

Repairing paths, drives and steps

Small cracks in the surface of a path or drive may point towards poor construction – weaknesses in the sub-base, for example, or faulty concrete mixing or misjudged curing times.

Before you start It is a waste of time to repair small cracks as soon as they appear. Wait to see if they increase in size and number. They may be caused by a small amount of movement in the ground below. If, after a year or so, there has been little or no increase, it is fair to assume that the ground has settled and repairs can be carried out. If the surface develops extensive cracking or sunken areas, take it up and lay it again on a new, firm sub-base.

Refitting a loose or damaged paving slab

1 Use a spade to chop through any mortar at edge joints. Push the spade under the slab to lift it and slip a broomstick or pipe under it to roll it out. A sunken or see-sawing slab can be re-laid, but renew a cracked or chipped slab.

2 If the slab was bedded on sand, loosen the old sand with a trowel, add more sharp sand, and lightly level the surface with a length of wood.

Alternatively If the slab was bedded on mortar, remove the old mortar with a hammer and chisel. Mix new bedding mortar in a dryish mix of one part cement

to four parts sharp sand (or use a bagged sand-cement mix) and spread it over the surface with a brick trowel to a thickness of 30–50mm. Roughen the surface with the trowel point.

MAKING A CONCRETE FILLER

Holes in a concrete path or step can be repaired. Prepare a cement and sharp sand mix in the proportions 1:3 by volume. For small amounts use a bagged sand-cement mix.

Separately mix equal parts of water and PVA adhesive – a building adhesive used to seal or bond various building materials is ideal.

Working on a board, gradually work the water and PVA adhesive into a pile of the dry materials. Mix until the filler is a smooth, moist consistency – neither crumbly nor too sloppy.

3 Slab edge joints may be flush or with gaps. If there are gaps, place 10mm thick wooden spacers along two adjacent edges before rolling the slab into position on a broomstick or pipe. Then even up the gaps.

4 Lay a 50mm thick piece of flat wood on the slab as a cushion while you use a club hammer to tap it down flush with the surrounding slabs. Check that it is flush using a length of straight-edged timber.

5 If you cannot tap the slab down flush, lift it again and skim off some of the bedding material. Or, if it sinks down too far, add more of the bedding material. Wait at least two days before filling in the joints.

DEALING WITH A DUST FILM

Light grey dust that forms continually on concrete and cannot be swept away is caused by the surface crumbling. It is usually the result of over-use of the float when smoothing the surface to a finish. Seal the surface by brushing on a priming coat of PVA adhesive and water as instructed on the container, usually with one part adhesive to five parts water.

Cleaning up stains

Oil, grease and rust stains, or moss, often occur on paths and drives. Most can be removed with one of the wide range of proprietary removers available from DIY, gardening or motoring stores. Cat litter is a good absorbent for spreading on fresh oil spillages.

Renewing damaged kerbing

1 Use a club hammer to loosen the damaged length of kerbing, then prise it out with a spade.

2 Dig out about 50mm of the sub-base below the removed kerbstone, then ram the surface well down with a thick piece of timber.

3 Mix bedding mortar using a bagged sand-cement mortar mix to a dryish consistency. Spread it about 75mm deep in the gap.

4 Dampen the new kerbstone and lower it into position. Cushion it with a 50mm piece of flat timber and tap it down with a club hammer until it is flush with the adjoining kerbstone.

5 Use a spirit level to check that the sides align with the adjoining kerbstone, and a straightedge to check that the surface is also aligned.

Repairing cracks or holes in concrete

Hairline cracks in concrete can be ignored. They often follow the lines of the contraction joints between sections.
• A hole can be filled if it is at least 15mm deep. If the hole is shallower, deepen it first, or the new layer will be too thin to hold firm.
• Repair concrete with a filler containing PVA adhesive (see box, page 61) to make a good bond.
• For potholes, proprietary ready-mixed concrete filler can be used instead.

1 Widen the crack or hole below the surface by undercutting the edges with a cold chisel and club hammer. This ensures that the filler will be well anchored.

2 Remove all debris from the hole or crack and brush it with a priming coat of PVA adhesive as instructed on the container – usually one part adhesive to five parts water.

3 When the priming coat is tacky, fill the crack or hole using concrete filler. Pack it well down so that there are no air pockets, which will weaken the concrete.

4 Level off the area flush with the surrounding surface using a brick trowel or plasterer's steel finishing trowel.

5 Keep the repair covered with polythene for at least three days.

Repairing crumbling edges on a concrete path

Concrete may crumble at the edges if the edging formwork was removed too soon, or if the wet concrete was not packed well down against the formwork during laying. Air pockets below an apparently solid surface cause the concrete to break up when the edges come under pressure during use.

1 Chip away the damaged concrete back to solid material, using a cold chisel and club hammer.

2 Remove the debris, and if the sub-base is exposed, ram the hardcore well down with a ramming tool or thick length of timber. Add fresh hardcore to any soft spots and ram it well down.

3 Set up timber edging 25mm thick alongside the damaged area so that the top edge is level with the concrete surface. Support it with pegs driven into the ground.

4 Brush the exposed edge of the concrete with a priming coat of PVA adhesive mixed according to the instructions on the container – usually one part adhesive to five parts water.

5 Prepare concrete filler (box, page 61) and use a brick trowel to press it firmly into the exposed area, well down against the edging.

6 Level the surface with the trowel, or use a float, to give a non-slip finish.

7 Cover the repaired area with polythene to stop it drying too fast. Remove the sheeting after three days. Leave the edging longer if the path is used a lot.

Repairing a concrete step

1 Cut back a crumbling edge using a cold chisel and club hammer. If the surface is worn down, score it with a brick bolster and hammer to provide a good grip (key) for a new layer of concrete.

2 Fix timber edging round the step using pegs and bricks to keep it firmly in place. If renewing a worn surface, set the edging about 15mm higher than the surface, with the side pieces allowing a forward slope of about 10mm for water to run off.

3 Brush away any dust and debris to give you a clean surface to work on.

4 Prime the area with a mixture of PVA adhesive and water according to the container instructions – usually one part adhesive to five parts water.

5 Repair crumbling edges with concrete filler (box, page 61). Press it well down against the edging.

Alternatively To re-surface the step, use bagged sand-cement mix prepared in the normal way, but first coat the surface with a solution of three parts PVA adhesive to one part water. Before it dries, apply the concrete to lie level with top of the edging.

6 Level the area. Cover for three days, as for path repairs.

GATES, PATHS AND DRIVES

The electrical system

Testing the wiring and electrical installations in a house is a job for a professional, but there are clues you can look for that will tell you that a system may be old and due for replacement.

If your home has an old wiring system, it may be unsafe. Check for these tell-tale signs.

Check the main fuse board

Look for cables from the meter going to a metal box with a main On/Off switch for the installation. There may be separate switched fuse boxes for each circuit. Inside the fuse boxes there may be circuit fuses in porcelain holders (below).

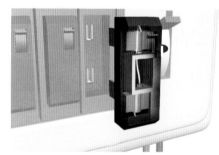

If your new home has an old-fashioned fuse box, consider getting it replaced with a modern consumer unit (opposite) containing miniature circuit breakers (MCBs). This is a relatively costly job, but it will make your electrics much safer and more convenient, as well as adding value to your home.

Old light switches

Round brass or Bakelite light switches mounted on wooden blocks are signs of a lighting system that is over 50 years old. The lighting circuits should be rewired with new cable and fittings as soon as possible.

Old wiring – new fittings

You may have a system where the old rubber-insulated cables remain, but the switches and sockets have been replaced by modern ones. Look at the circuit cables where they emerge from the fuse box. If you find old cables, have them checked by an electrician, and plan to have the system rewired as soon as possible.

Round-pin sockets

If you have old-style round-pin sockets, your wiring system is likely to be 50 or more years old. It should be completely rewired without delay for safety reasons.

Modern wiring systems

A modern house or one that has been rewired or updated will have a consumer unit (right) in place of the old-fashioned fuse box.

The consumer unit This houses the main on-off switch, the earthing terminal block for all the house circuits and individual fuses or miniature circuit breakers (MCBs) for each separate circuit. Some units have blanked-off spaces for additional MCBs to be installed at a later date.

Lighting and power circuits will be connected to separate MCBs and there should be a dedicated circuit for an electric cooker. Label the MCBs to show which circuit each one protects. To identify the circuits, turn off the main switch and switch off one MCB at a time. Turn the main switch back on and check which lights or appliances are not working.

Residual current device (RCD) An RCD monitors the balance of the live and neutral current flows. An imbalance occurs if current leaks from a circuit because of faulty insulation, or because someone has touched a live part and received an electric shock. If the RCD detects an imbalance, it switches off the supply immediately – fast enough to prevent an electric shock from being fatal.

• An RCD is installed to protect only at-risk circuits such as those to socket outlets and some stand-alone appliances.

• An RCD in its own enclosure may have been added to an existing installation to protect new at-risk circuits.

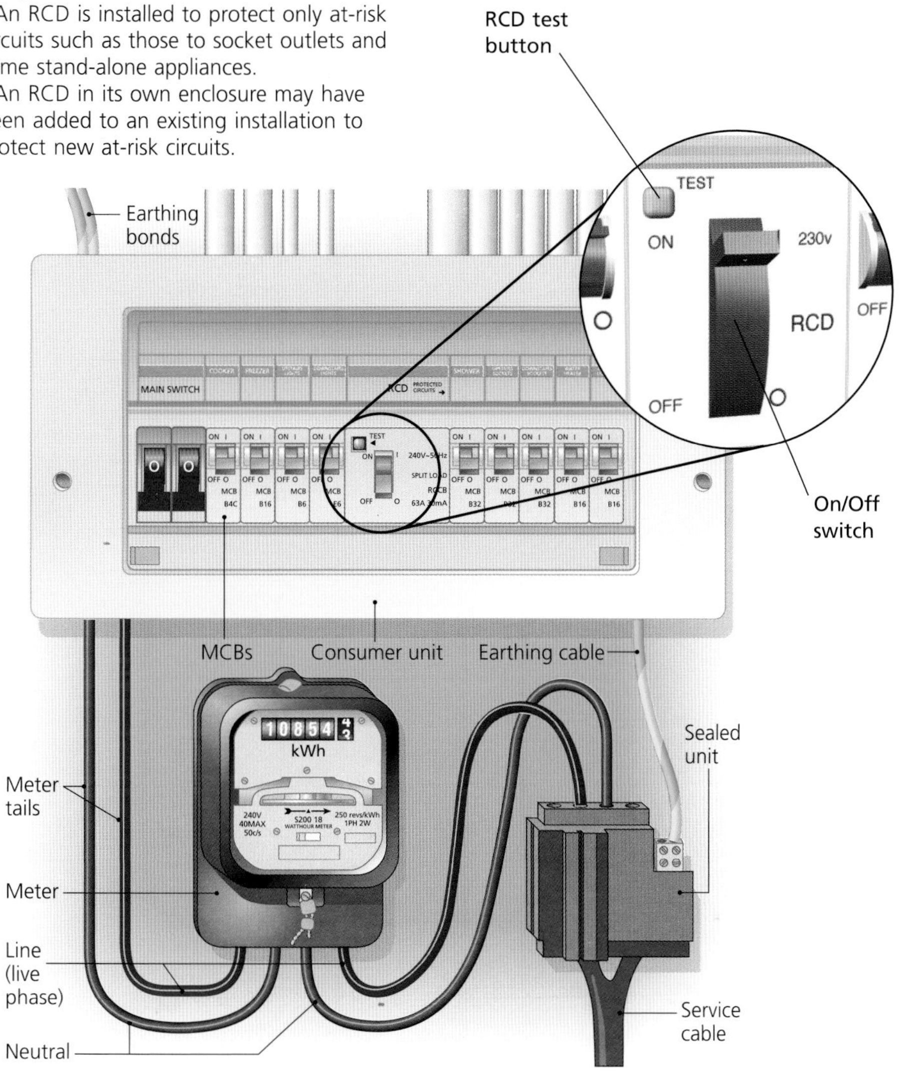

RCD test button

TEST

ON 230v

RCD OFF

OFF

On/Off switch

Earthing bonds

MAIN SWITCH

MCBs   Consumer unit   Earthing cable

Sealed unit

Meter tails

Meter

Line (live phase)

Neutral

Service cable

WIRING REGULATIONS

Since January 2005, all new domestic wiring work in England and Wales must comply with the requirements of a new section of the Building Regulations. Part P, entitled Electrical Safety, covers the design, installation, inspection and testing of electrical work in the home. It applies to both professional and DIY electrical work.

What you need to know:

1 You can still do your own wiring work, but it must be inspected, tested and certified by a professional electrician.

2 Any minor work that is not on a fixed electrical installation (for example, lamps and other appliances that can be unplugged) does not need approval.

3 You must notify your local authority building control department before you start major wiring jobs and pay a fee for inspection and testing when the job is completed.

The gas supply

Never attempt to carry out any work or maintenance on your gas supply pipes or any gas appliances.

Be alert for very old-looking gas fires and boilers. They may be a sign that the gas supply to the home is outdated and may not have been regularly maintained. When doing work on a house you may unearth old gas pipes in the walls or ceilings. These would have been used to supply gas lamps. Always check with a professional before cutting or removing them.

Find and check your stoptap

Locate the stoptap for your gas supply when you first move in to a house and make sure that it turns freely. The gas tap is normally near the meter. You will need to be able to turn off the supply in the event of an emergency, so it is vital that the tap has not seized in the open position.

Set up regular services
All boilers, gas fires and any other gas appliances in the home should be serviced annually. Faulty appliances can give off dangerous carbon monoxide, which cannot be detected by smell.

SAFETY WARNING

The Gas Safety (Installation and Use) Regulations make it illegal for anyone who is not 'competent' to carry out work relating to gas supply and fittings. This means leaving all work on your gas supply and equipment to a qualified gas fitter, registered with CORGI (The Council for Registered Gas Installers).

The water and central heating systems

The age of a house determines the type of systems in place. They should be regularly maintained to keep them in good working order.

Make sure that you and others in the house know where the indoor and outdoor stoptaps are, as well as the gatevalves on the supply pipes to the hot water cylinder and cold taps, and label them. Check all stoptaps once a year to make sure that they turn freely.

The cold water supply

There are two types of cold water supply in British homes: direct and indirect.

In a direct cold water supply, branch pipes from the rising main lead directly to all the cold taps and WC cisterns in the house. This means that you can drink cold water from any tap. A pipe from the rising main will usually feed a storage cistern in the loft – the reservoir that feeds the hot water cylinder. A direct cold water system is simpler and cheaper to install than an indirect system.

Most British homes have an indirect system. The rising main feeds the cold tap at the kitchen sink (and possibly pipes to a washing machine and an outside tap). This water is clean drinking water. It then continues up to a cold water storage tank in the roof, which supplies all other taps, the WCs and the hot water cylinder.

SAFETY NOTE

If your house has an indirect system, do not drink water from any tap other than the kitchen one. Water from a tank may not be clean.

The hot water supply

There are two basic hot water systems: indirect, with all hot taps supplied from a hot water storage cylinder, or direct, where cold water is heated on demand. The latter is usual when all the cold water supplies come direct from the rising main.

Back boilers and separate kitchen boilers have largely been replaced by modern boilers that supply both hot water and central heating.

Instantaneous hot water systems

Single point water heaters may be heated by gas or electricity and are usually sited next to the point they serve. In the case of electric heaters, such as a shower, they must be wired to the mains via an isolating switch. Many homes are now being fitted with multipoint water heaters – most commonly combination (combi) boilers. A combi boiler combines the functions of a central heating boiler and an instantaneous multipoint water heater.

Indirect systems

You can identify an indirect system by the two water tanks in the loft. The second, smaller one, has a vent pipe over the top. This is called a header tank, or feed-and-expansion tank. It maintains the level of water in the primary circuit, where water heated by the boiler is passed through a coil in the hot water cylinder to heat the water stored inside. The level of water in the header tank is low enough to allow the water to rise as it expands when it gets hot. The main cold water cistern supplies water to the hot water cylinder, topping it up as water is drawn off through the taps.

Unvented (sealed) hot water systems

This system is the same as an indirect system, except that it is connected to the mains. This gives mains water pressure to hot taps and showers. Many safety features are built into this type of system to allow for the greater pressure and expansion of the water. No cold water storage cistern or header tank is needed, so there is no pipework in the loft.

Direct systems

In older houses with a direct system (often back boilers or solid-fuel boilers), the water is heated directly by circulation through the boiler. Water is fed from the cold water cistern into the bottom of the cylinder and then to the boiler. The flow pipe from the top of the boiler discharges hot water directly into the top of the cylinder, forcing colder, denser water at the bottom through the return pipe back to the boiler. The hottest water, being the lightest, is always at the top ready to be drawn off.

Immersion heater

This is another form of direct heating. The hot water cylinder can be heated by one or two electric immersion heaters. About 1kW of heat is needed for every 45 litres of water, so a 140-litre hot water cylinder needs a 3kW heater. Today, an immersion heater is rarely the sole form of water heating in the home. Rather, it is used to supplement a boiler system or as a way to heat water in summer when the central heating boiler is switched off.

Waste water

If you live in a house built before the mid-1960s, you probably have a two pipe drainage system (see diagram, page 68), where waste from upstairs WCs and from baths and basins are carried to the main drains via separate pipes, or soil stacks, on the outside wall of the house. Newer houses have one drain pipe – a single stack system – to carry all the waste.

Whatever the system, every bath, basin or sink in the house is fitted with a trap – a bend in the outlet pipe below the plughole. This holds sufficient water to stop gases from the drains entering the house and causing an unpleasant smell. The trap has some means of access for clearing blockages. All WC pans have built-in traps.

Central heating

In some older central heating systems and in solid fuel systems, water is circulated by gravity, relying on the principle that hot water expands as it heats, and weighs less than cold water. Tell-tale signs that you have a gravity-fed system are large 28mm central heating pipes.

Modern systems circulate water to radiators with a pump. The same water is constantly circulated around the system through the boiler, to the radiators and back. In an open system, water from a feed-and-expansion cistern in the loft tops up the system in case of leakage or evaporation. This cistern allows for the water in the system to expand when it is hot. Sealed systems incorporate an expansion vessel for this purpose instead of a cistern in the loft. The water must be topped up from the mains supply from time to time and after any work has been done on the radiator network. Sealed systems are ideal for flats, where it can be difficult to find space for tanks.

Common plumbing and heating faults

The plumbing system

Your plumbing system can suffer from a wide range of faults, but they fall into four main categories.

Taps and valves ❶

Taps and valves control the flow of water into and through the home. They may drip, causing stains and overflows, or may jam open or closed, or be hard to operate. Taps might need maintenance or replacement, depending on the severity of the problem.

Supply pipes ❷

Supply pipes distribute water to wherever it is needed. They may leak, due to perforations developing in the pipe or faulty seals at pipe connectors. They may also gradually become blocked by scale, caused by hard water. Both faults are easily remedied, although leaks demand swift damage limitation – see Plumbing emergency action (right).

Storage tanks ❸

Storage tanks hold cold and hot water. They may develop leaks or, in the case of the hot tank, may become inefficient due to a build-up of limescale. Replacement is the only long-term solution.

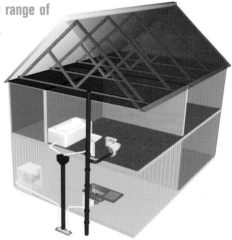

Waste pipes

Waste pipes (above) convey used water from appliances and WCs to the household drains, via U-shaped traps designed to keep drain smells out of the house. They can become blocked, causing overflows, but most blockages can be cleared easily.

PLUMBING EMERGENCY ACTION

■ If a fault causes water to escape, aim to stop the flow as quickly as possible.

■ Make sure you know in advance where the system's main on/off and flow controls are located (see page 12).

■ Empty leaking water storage tanks and supply pipes by turning off the main stoptap and opening cold taps (see page 29), or by attaching a garden hose to a drain valve and opening the valve with pliers or a spanner. Lead the hose outside the house.

■ Clear blocked waste pipes and traps by dismantling, plunging or rodding (see page 34).

The heating system

A central heating system consists of five main components, each of which can malfunction or fail.

The boiler ❶

The boiler heats the system (and may also provide domestic hot water). It contains a number of parts that will need regular maintenance and eventual replacement and this is a job for a professional (see page 66). Annual servicing will keep the boiler in good order.

The pump ❷

The pump circulates heated water round the system. It may become jammed or noisy in operation, or may simply fail altogether. Regular operation and cleaning help to prevent problems, but replacement is usually straightforward.

The radiators ❸

The radiators transmit heat to individual rooms. They sometimes develop pinhole leaks due to corrosion, and may trap air, gas or sludge (by-products of corrosion), all of which can cause uneven heating or banging noises when in use. The use of a corrosion inhibitor or leak sealer will help to prevent or cure these problems. Leaks require prompt action.

The header tank ❹

The header tank (also called the feed-and-expansion tank) tops up any water lost from the heating system through leaks or evaporation. The tank itself may also develop a leak and need replacing. The ballvalve that refills it may jam through lack of use, causing an overflow or allowing air to be drawn into the radiators and pump. A ballvalve can be repaired or replaced.

The controls ❺

Controls operating the heating system include a programmer, thermostats and motorised valves. Faulty wiring may lead to malfunction, and mechanical failure may be remedied through servicing or replacement of the faulty control.

HEATING EMERGENCY ACTION

■ If the system overheats or the pump fails, turn off the boiler.
■ Turn off the gas at the meter immediately if you smell a gas leak and call the Transco gas emergency number (0800 111 999).
■ Until you can make a repair, drain leaking pipes, radiators and hot water cylinders via the relevant drain cock.

Sealed systems

The essential components of a sealed system are now usually housed inside the boiler. As well as saving space because of the lack of a feed-and-expansion cistern, a combination boiler also has the advantage that no hot water cylinder is needed as the boiler heats mains water and delivers hot water directly to the taps. This minimises the range of problems that may occur with the heating system.

Interior

Internal walls and ceilings

Internal walls contribute significantly to the stability of the building, and may support the structure of the storey above. Inspect them closely for faults or signs of weakness.

The way internal walls are built depends largely on the age of the house, and knowing about their structure can affect how you carry out DIY work on them.

Internal partitions

You can discover what type of partition walls you have by tapping the wall surface to see if it is solid or hollow, and then following this with test-drilling to reveal the materials used to construct it.

Brick walls In most properties built before the 1930s, internal partitions in ground-floor rooms are generally of brickwork, one brick thick, built in stretcher bond. With plaster on both faces, they are about 140mm thick overall. They support the floor joists of first-floor rooms, and most of them are load-bearing. At least one of these walls will continue into the first storey (and higher in multi-storey houses), and will help to carry the load of the roof structure. Bear this in mind if you are considering removing walls to alter room layouts.

Block walls In properties built later than about 1930, 100mm thick concrete blockwork is used in ground-floor load-bearing partitions and, again, these may be extended into upper storeys to support the roof structure. The plaster is generally thinner (and harder) than on old brick partitions, so the walls will measure about 125mm thick. You may also find non-loadbearing blockwork partitions, which are built in thinner blockwork.

To confirm whether you have brick or block partition walls drill three holes in an equilateral triangle, each hole about 50mm from the others; this guarantees that at least one hole will miss a mortar joint. Brick dust will be reddish or yellowish, whereas block dust will be grey or black.

Timber stud partitions Timber-framed walls, built with 100 x 50mm or 75 x 50mm sawn timber, are used as internal partitions in houses of all ages. The vertical studs are fixed at regular intervals (commonly 400mm) between a timber head plate nailed to the ceiling joists and a corresponding sole plate fixed to the floor. Horizontal noggings are fitted between the studs to stiffen the structure.

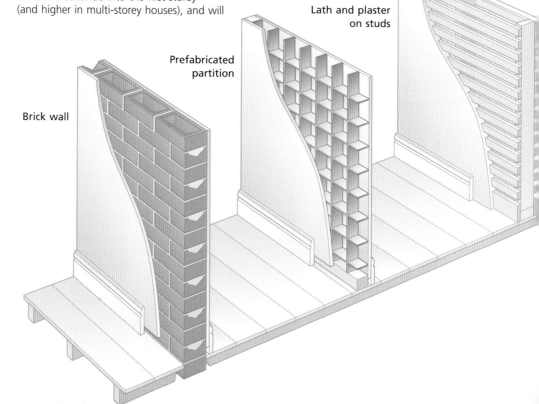

Lath and plaster on studs

Prefabricated partition

Brick wall

Timber stud partitions may be load-bearing, although partitions in upper floor rooms are usually not, especially if their position does not coincide with a partition in the floor below. As a general rule, partitions of 75 x 50mm timber are never load-bearing. The framework will be clad in lath and plaster up to 20mm thick in older houses, and in 9.5 or 12.7mm thick plasterboard in those built since the late 1940s. A single test drilling will instantly reveal the type of cladding you have.

In houses built since the late 1960s, the roof structure is generally built using trussed rafters, which span the external walls of the house and do away with the need for load-bearing partition walls in upper floors. In houses with this type of roof structure, all upstairs partitions are timber-framed.

Prefabricated partitions In houses built in the last 20 years or so, you may encounter internal partitions built using prefabricated

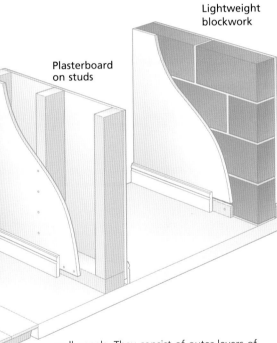

Lightweight blockwork

Plasterboard on studs

wall panels. They consist of outer layers of plasterboard bonded to a cardboard core of egg-box construction, and are 1200mm wide and 50mm thick. The panels rest on a timber sole plate and are fixed to timber battens at each end and at panel junctions.

Openings in partitions

In old internal brick partitions, door openings are commonly spanned by stout timber beams. Blockwork partitions have openings spanned by short lintels, of

reinforced concrete or galvanised steel. Openings in timber-framed partition walls are suitably spaced between a pair of vertical studs, with the sole plate cut away and a cross-piece fixed between the studs to create the door head.

The opening is lined with a timber frame fixed to the masonry or the wall studs. The joint between wall surface and door frame is covered by an architrave moulding.

THE TROUBLE WITH PARTITIONS

Apart from the usual (and expected) problems of superficial damage to the plaster or plasterboard surfaces of the wall, partitions can suffer from structural problems. The most serious is settlement of solid walls, caused by inadequate support being provided for the wall when it was built, or by subsequent ground movement. This causes cracks in the wall and at junctions with the ceiling and other walls, and doors may become difficult to shut as the frames are distorted. Settlement can also be caused by load-bearing walls being overloaded if the original roof covering has been replaced with a heavier material.

Lateral movement in solid walls can result from inadequate tying of the partitions to the external walls of the house during construction. In timber-framed walls, such movement is usually due to shrinkage of the timber frame, which may result from the use of poorly stored timber on a wet building site.

What to do
Superficial damage to wall surfaces can be repaired easily on a DIY basis (see page 75). Settlement of solid walls usually requires some form of underpinning, and is a job for a surveyor to assess and an underpinning specialist to carry out. Lateral movement can often be cured by introducing lateral ties between the affected parts of the structure – again work for an expert. Shrinkage in timber-framed walls will cease once the wood has dried out, and the resulting cracks can then be filled and concealed.

Ceilings

There is much less variation in the construction of ceilings, compared with partition walls. Once again, the age of the house is the key to the method used.

Ceilings are probably the most neglected surface in the house. They get little more than the most perfunctory decoration compared with walls, floors and woodwork, and tend to get noticed only when they start to cause trouble. However, they are a very good indicator of when things are going wrong. Check your ceilings regularly for sagging, damp marks and stains. Cracks in a plastered ceiling should be checked and monitored, to see if they worsen.

Lath and plaster Until the use of plasterboard became commonplace after the 1940s, ceilings were formed of lath and plaster in the same way as timber stud partition walls. Split or sawn timber laths 25–40mm wide and up to 13mm thick were nailed to the undersides of the ceiling joists, spaced about 10mm apart. The first coat of plaster was then applied and forced up between the laths to provide a fixing key. You can see these plaster ridges clearly if you view the ceiling surface from above – in a loft, for example. After the first coat had dried, two further coats of plaster were then applied to give a ceiling thickness of up to about 25mm.

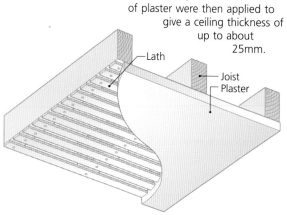

Lath and plaster ceiling

Timber You may come across boarded ceilings in unrestored Victorian houses, especially in cellars and basement rooms. These consist of tongued-and-grooved boards nailed directly to the ceiling joists. They were generally gloss-painted.

Plasterboard Ceilings in modern houses consist of sheets of 9.5mm plasterboard nailed to the ceiling joists, and to noggings fixed between the joists to support the board ends. The joints between the boards are taped to prevent movement cracks from developing, and the plasterboard is either skim-coated with plaster or decorated directly – often with a textured coating such as Artex.

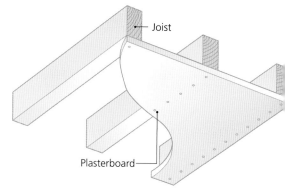

Plasterboard ceiling

THE TROUBLE WITH CEILINGS

Lath and plaster ceilings often fail with age because of the loss of the key between the plaster and the laths. Plasterboard ceilings may crack along the board joints, especially if these were not properly taped during installation. Both types can be holed by physical damage, and are badly affected by plumbing leaks. Minor leaks can cause staining which is difficult to conceal, and major ones can cause the ceiling to collapse.

What to do

Minor damage to any ceiling can be patched with plaster or plasterboard. Old lath and plaster ceilings in poor condition are best replaced with a new plasterboard ceiling. See page 80 for details of the work involved.

Patching damaged plaster

Large cracks, holes or crumbling areas of plaster can generally be repaired quickly and cheaply with plaster.

Do not repair damage caused by damp until the cause has been remedied. If large cracks reopen after repair, seek the advice of a builder or surveyor, as the cracks may be caused by structural movement of the building.

Using ready-mixed plaster

Tools *Cold chisel; club hammer; hand brush; filling knife or plasterer's trowel. Possibly also fine abrasive paper or power sander; face mask and safety goggles; large paintbrush; plastic spreader (supplied with skim-coat container).*

Materials *Ready-mixed plaster. Possibly ready-mixed skim-coat plaster.*

1 Chip away loose or crumbling plaster with a cold chisel until you reach a firm surface all round.

2 Brush away dust and debris. If bricks or building blocks are exposed, dampen the areas with water.

3 Stir the plaster and apply it to the wall with a filling knife or plasterer's trowel held at an angle.

4 Build up deep areas in layers – applied up to 50mm deep in cavities. Allow each layer to stiffen before applying the next.

5 If the surface is to be papered, fill the undercoat to the top of the damaged area. When it is thoroughly dry, smooth it with fine abrasive paper or a power sander. Wear a mask and goggles to protect you from dust.

Alternatively If the surface is to be painted, fill the top 3mm of the area with a coat of skim plaster to give a smooth finish, applied with a large brush. When it begins to dry, smooth it with the plastic spreader supplied.

Repairing and reinforcing corners

When filling an external corner with plaster, it can be difficult to get a level surface and a straight edge. The job is easier if it is done in two operations using a timber batten as a guide.

Tools *Cold chisel; club hammer; softwood timber batten 50 x 20mm and longer than the depth of the area to be filled; straight-edge; masonry nails; hammer; hand brush; plasterer's trowel. Possibly also carrying board; large paintbrush or plant spray; spirit level with horizontal and vertical vials; corner trowel; rubber gloves.*

Materials *Plaster.*

1 Cut back crumbling plaster to a firm surface and brush away debris from the damaged area.

2 Drive two masonry nails through the batten, closer to one edge than the other, and position them so that they will either be driven into the mortar between bricks, or will fit into firm plaster well beyond the edges of the damaged area.

3 Hold the timber batten vertically against the damaged edge with the nails nearer to the inner side. Use a straight-edge along the adjacent wall to align the batten with the plaster surface at the top and bottom.

4 Nail the batten gently to the wall, leaving the nail heads protruding.

5 Plaster the area with a suitable undercoat or one-coat plaster to align with the edge of the batten.

6 When the plaster has dried, remove the nails and pull away the batten to avoid crumbling the edge of the new plaster.

7 Nail the batten to the other side of the corner and then plaster the remaining damaged area in the same way.

8 If using a finishing coat, use the batten in the same way to plaster both sides of the corner.

9 Finishing the edge of the corner is easier with a corner trowel. Or you could round it off with a plasterer's trowel.

Alternatively Before the plaster hardens fully, put on a rubber glove, wet it, and run your fingers down the edge to blunt it slightly.

Repairs around sockets

1 Switch off the mains supply at the consumer unit before patching round a switch or socket.

2 Disconnect the fitting, noting the wiring connections, and remove it.

3 Whether the socket is seated in plaster or plasterboard, fill small cracks or holes with an interior filler and larger holes by one of the methods described above.

4 Wait for the plaster to dry before refitting the switch or socket.

Repairs around ceiling roses and light fittings

1 Turn off the mains supply at the consumer unit when dealing with light fittings. Repairs to the edge of a ceiling rose generally do not carry any risk of electric shock.

2 For small, difficult to reach holes and breaks in the plaster, use a small amount of expanding foam filler.

3 Squirt some filler into the space.

4 Allow it to harden and then cut away the excess with a sharp knife.

Filling gaps round waste pipes

When a new dishwasher or washing machine is fitted, it may be necessary to make a hole through the wall, to accommodate the water waste pipes.

Once the pipe is fitted, it is necessary to fill the space around the pipe in order to cut down on draughts and to prevent damp from entering the property.

Squirt expanding foam filler all round the pipe and allow it to dry thoroughly before trimming off the excess with a sharp knife. The advantage of this material is that it can be removed quite easily should you wish to move the appliance to another position.

Filling holes in lath and plaster

Fill minor damage in the same way as for ordinary plaster. If the damage reveals the laths, repair depends on whether the laths are intact or broken.

If the laths are intact

Paint the laths with a solution of PVA adhesive to make the surface less absorbent. Fill the hole with layers of plaster (page 75). If you are using ordinary quick-setting plaster, use a bonding under-coat plaster.

If the laths are broken

Either patch the laths or – if the hole is not more than about 75mm across – plug the gap before you fill it with plaster.

To patch the laths, use a piece of expanded metal mesh, cut to the size you need with tinsnips. Wrap it round the laths to bridge the gap between broken edges.

Alternatively To plug the gap, use a ball of newspaper soaked in water and then worked round in a bowl of runny plaster.

Dealing with large areas

1 Where a large area of plaster has come away, cut back the damage to a regular shape and patch it with a piece of plasterboard. Use plasterboard that is as close to the thickness of the plaster as possible. Nail the patch, ivory side outwards, to the timber frame that supports the laths.

REINFORCING A DAMAGED CORNER

If an external corner is prone to damage, reinforce it with expanded metal angle beading. Treat cut ends and any areas damaged during installation with metal primer.

1 Fit beading against the corner with dabs of plaster about 600mm apart on each side. Use a straight-edge and spirit level to make sure it is vertical.

2 Press the mesh firmly against the wall and check with a straight-edge that the corner bead will not protrude above the plaster surface.

3 Use the bead instead of a timber batten as a guide to forming a straight edge when plastering.

2 Fill the gaps round the edges with interior filler and finish the surface with a coat of skim plaster.

Repairing holes in plasterboard

Small holes in plasterboard can be repaired in the same way as in plaster. Medium-sized holes – up to about 125mm across – need to be fitted with a backing piece to block the cavity before they are filled with plaster filler. Larger holes, or a severely damaged surface, cannot be satisfactorily repaired with a filler. The damaged section must be removed and a new piece of plasterboard patched in.

Using a backing piece

Tools *Pencil and ruler; trimming knife; drill and twist bit; padsaw or mini hacksaw; filling knife; sanding block; scissors; length of wood.*

Materials *A plasterboard offcut or a piece of MDF; piece of string 150–200mm long; a long nail or wood sliver; interior or plaster filler or coving adhesive. Possibly finishing plaster.*

1 Draw a neat square around the damaged area, and drill holes at the corners so that you can get the blade of your padsaw in. Cut along the lines to create a neat, straight-sided hole.

2 Cut a backing piece from a plasterboard offcut. It should be narrow enough to go through the hole, but long enough to overlap the hole by about 25mm at the top and bottom.

3 Bore a hole in the middle of the backing piece and thread the length of string through it.

4 Knot a nail or a sliver of wood to one end of the string to anchor it against the back of the offcut. Make sure you have the ivory side as the front. Make a loop in the front end of the string so that it is easy to hold.

5 Apply coving adhesive or filler to the front (the ivory side) of the backing piece.

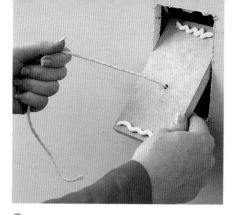

6 Guide the coated backing piece through the hole, then use the string to pull it into position against the back of the hole.

7 The patch should stick fairly quickly. Cut off the string when you are sure it has stuck firmly.

8 Use quick-setting filler to cover the patch, filling the hole to about half its depth. When it has dried, put in another layer, leaving it slightly proud of the surrounding wall.

9 With a length of wood, skim off the excess filler, leaving a smooth surface level with the surrounding area.

10 When the filler has dried completely, smooth the surface with a sanding block or a piece of fine abrasive paper.

HELPFUL TIP

If the surface of your plasterboard wall is dented but not broken, simply cover the dent with quick-setting filler and smooth it level with a ruler. Once it is dry, sand it smooth and redecorate.

Fitting a plasterboard patch

Tools *Trimming knife or padsaw; broad-bladed filling knife or plasterer's trowel; pencil; straight-edge; spirit level; try square; hammer; medium or fine abrasive paper; sponge; steel tape measure.*

Materials *Small sheet of plasterboard or offcut as thick as board on wall; two lengths of timber to fit tightly between uprights (studs) – you will need the 50 x 75mm size for a stud-partition wall or 50 x 25mm for a dry-lined wall; four 75mm oval nails; 30mm galvanised plasterboard nails; G-cramps; joint tape or scrim tape; joint compound or plasterboard finishing plaster.*

1 Check that there are no pipes or cables behind the board. Use a trimming knife or padsaw to cut across the plasterboard from the middle of the damaged area outwards to each side until you reach the timber studs supporting the panel.

2 Use the straight edge of a spirit level to draw the edge line of the studs vertically on the plasterboard. Then draw horizontal parallel lines across the panel between the studs, about 50mm above and below the edge of the damaged area. Make sure the lines are at right angles to the studs.

3 Cut out the squared-off section of damaged plasterboard.

4 On each side of the opening, draw a vertical line to indicate half the width of the timber stud and score it using a straight-edge and trimming knife.

5 Cut back the sound plasterboard down the scored lines to reveal half the width of the studs.

6 Fit the two timber pieces as cross-pieces (noggings) between the studs at the top and bottom of the opening. Position them with the 50mm thick side outwards so 25mm is under the edge of the existing plasterboard as a nailing surface for the patch.

7 Hold the noggins in position with G-cramps while you drive 75mm oval nails through the noggins and into the studs at an angle.

8 Measure the area of the hole and cut plasterboard to fit. Insert it with the ivory side facing outwards so that it can be plastered or decorated.

9 Nail the plasterboard to the wood surround with plasterboard nails. Set the nails 150mm apart, positioned at least 12mm from the edge of the patch. Sink them into the surface of the plasterboard so they do not protrude, but take care not to damage the outer layer of paper.

10 Lightly sand edges of the joint with abrasive paper to remove any burring.

11 Using a plasterboard finishing plaster or joint compound, fill the joints and sand them smooth and flat.

Repairing ceilings

Modern ceilings are generally made of plasterboard, but lath-and-plaster ceilings are still found in some older houses. To reach the ceiling easily and safely, with your head about 150mm from it, use either the base section of a scaffold tower or stout scaffold boards resting on two stepladders or hired decorator's trestles.

Gaps where wall and ceiling meet

The simplest way to cover gaps between the wall and ceiling is to fit coving – decorative moulding specially designed for wall and ceiling joints. A less effective alternative is to seal the gap with acrylic decorator's sealant.

Dealing with a bulge in the ceiling

On a lath-and-plaster ceiling, an area of plaster may sag away from the laths to form a bulge. If you can get at the ceiling from above you may be able to repair it.

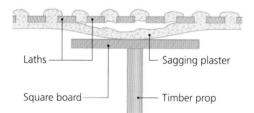

Laths — — Sagging plaster

Square board — — Timber prop

1 Try to push the bulge back into position using a square of chipboard or plywood nailed to a floor-to-ceiling timber prop.

2 To re-fix the plaster, you need to reach it from above – either from the loft or by lifting the floorboards in the room above.

3 Vacuum clean the area between the joists at the back of the ceiling bulge.

4 Pour fairly runny bonding plaster over the area. This should bond the ceiling plaster back to the laths, replacing the 'nibs' of holding plaster that have been broken or dislodged.

PULLING DOWN AN OLD CEILING

It is best to replace an old lath-and-plaster ceiling with a plasterboard one if it needs more than small localised repairs. If the plaster key has failed in one place already, it is sure to fail in others as time goes by. However, this is an extremely dusty and unpleasant job.

Prepare by clearing the room of all furniture and fittings, and lift any carpet and its underlay. Remove ceiling-mounted light fittings and insert the cable conductors into plastic terminal blocks before pushing the cable up into the ceiling void. Hire enough heavy-duty dust sheets to cover the entire floor, and invest in safety goggles, strong work gloves, a supply of disposable face masks and a cap. Wear old clothes or a disposable one-piece work suit. Set up a work platform spanning the room, using stepladders or trestles and scaffold boards. Tape up the room door to keep the dust in, and open all the windows. Put on your safety gear.

It is best to pull down the old ceiling from below, even if you have access from above via a loft, because this way you can keep the demolition under better control.

Start by making a hole in the old ceiling with a club hammer, and tear down the old plaster and the laths section by section, working parallel to the joists. A small crowbar is an ideal tool to use for this. Try to pile the debris in one corner of the room as you work.

When you have pulled down as much of the ceiling as possible, work along each joist in turn, removing any remaining pieces of lath and pulling out all the old nails. Then finish by brushing the sides and bottom of each joist with a stiff brush to remove any remaining debris.

5 Leave the supporting prop in place until the plaster has dried. If this method does not work, remove the sagging area and patch it with plasterboard. A ceiling that sags over a large area should be pulled down and replaced.

Ground floors

The age of a house will determine the construction of its ground floor. Whether made of rammed earth, concrete or timber, damp and rot are the major problems to look for.

In the oldest houses, the earth beneath the house was simply levelled and covered with flagstones. Solid floors like these were notoriously damp and extremely cold. Only slate kept the dampness out. During the early 19th century, asphalt was introduced to form a damp-proof layer, and quarry and ceramic tiles became widespread as a finished surface. But the Victorians acknowledged the difficulty of damp-proofing solid floors effectively, and turned to timber as an alternative. Properly constructed, these floors were not only free from damp; they were also warmer underfoot. However, they were prone to rot, and solid concrete ground floors are once again the norm in modern houses.

Timber ground floors

A traditional timber ground floor is supported on joists. The ground beneath the floor is covered with a layer of concrete (oversite concrete). The ends of the joists are either fitted directly into holes left in the brickwork or are supported on (and nailed to) a horizontal timber wall plate resting on a ledge of masonry. The resulting underfloor void (called the crawl space) is a minimum of 300mm deep, and often more.

THE TROUBLE WITH TIMBER FLOORS

If the ventilation of the underfloor void is inadequate, the structure will often become plagued by dry rot, a ravenous form of wood-destroying fungus which can eventually cause its total collapse.

Joist ends are prone to attacks of wet rot, which are often linked to localised failures in the damp-proof course in the house walls. Another problem is that the void can be invaded by rodents and other pests, which use it as an easy access route into the house itself.

What to do

Make sure that the void is well ventilated by keeping airbricks clear of obstructions. Replace damaged airbricks to deny pests entry. If the floor appears springy at the edges, wet rot may be affecting the joist ends. It may be possible to reinforce them with new wood, but large-scale replacement of the floor structure may be necessary.

If there is a tell-tale musty smell in ground-floor rooms and you find dry rot, the entire floor structure will have to be replaced and the area sterilised before a new floor is constructed. Both these jobs are best left to specialist contractors.

Minor faults involving damage to floorboards can be repaired by a competent do-it-yourselfer (see pages 84–86).

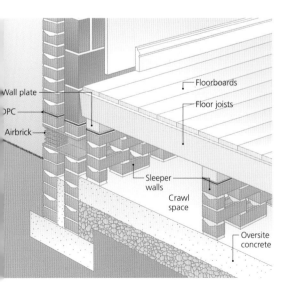

Wall plate
DPC
Airbrick
Floorboards
Floor joists
Sleeper walls
Crawl space
Oversite concrete

A damp-proof course (DPC) between the wall plate and the masonry protects the timber from damp. Intermediate supports called sleeper walls are built up off the oversite concrete at roughly 3m intervals to prevent the joists from sagging across large spans. These are of honeycomb construction to allow air movement through the underfloor void – essential to keep the floor timbers dry and free from rot. They also carry a wall plate (resting on a DPC) to which the joists are nailed.

The floor surface is formed of softwood boards which are nailed to the joists. These were made from square-edged boards up until the 1930s, and generally tongued-and-grooved thereafter. Square-edged boards became unpopular because they usually shrank and created gaps, which caused draughts.

Modern solid ground floors

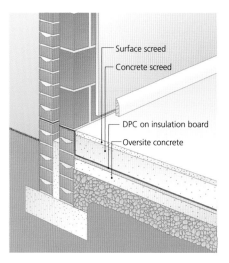

Surface screed
Concrete screed

DPC on insulation board
Oversite concrete

By the end of the 19th century, it had become obvious that timber ground floors caused more problems than they solved, and a solid floor – waterproofed initially with asphalt and later with heavy-duty plastic membranes – once again became the norm in house construction.

These floors consist of a bed of rammed hardcore, filled with sand (a process known as blinding) and topped by a layer of concrete 100–150mm thick. A damp-proof membrane (DPM), sometimes called a damp-proof course (DOC) is laid over the concrete, and a further screeding layer of mortar or fine concrete up to 63mm thick

THE TROUBLE WITH SOLID FLOORS

The commonest problem with solid ground floors is a failed DPM. This can usually be remedied by sealing the floor slab with a liquid damp-proofer, covered with a new thin surface screed (see page 87).

Damp may also be caused by leaks in buried plumbing or heating pipes, which will have to be excavated and repaired. It is possible to hire a concrete breaker (with vibration damping) to do this job yourself. Wear protective clothing and goggles, and make sure you know where water and gas pipes have been laid.

An uneven concrete floor can be treated with a self-smoothing compound which will raise the floor level by about 10mm.

is added to form the final floor surface.

The latest Building Regulations require solid floors to be insulated, and the structure now includes a thick layer of rigid polystyrene or other foam insulation. This is placed between the hardcore and the concrete.

Another recent development is the use of suspended concrete ground floors, mainly on sloping sites where a solid infill would be prohibitively expensive. The floor is formed by inverted T-shaped beams of reinforced concrete that span the underfloor void, like traditional timber floor joists. Insulating concrete blocks rest on the flanges of the beams to form the floor slab, which is then topped with insulation and a fine screed as for solid floors.

Upper floors

Two and three-storey houses invariably have upper floors supported on timber joists. These span individual rooms and are supported by load-bearing walls between rooms on the ground floor.

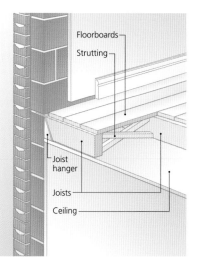

Floorboards
Strutting

Joist hanger
Joists
Ceiling

In older houses, the joist ends rest either in sockets in the outer walls, or on ledges in the masonry if the wall thickness decreases as the storeys rise.

In more modern buildings, they are supported by metal joist hangers built into the masonry. The joists are usually deeper (up to 230mm) than those in a suspended timber ground floor because they often have no intermediate supports.

Stairwell opening in first floor

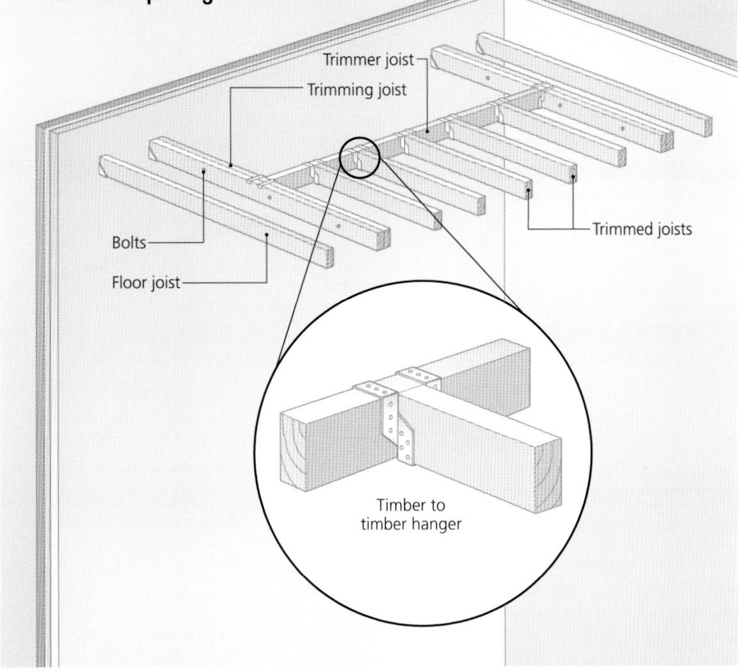

Trimmer joist

Trimming joist

Bolts

Floor joist

Trimmed joists

Timber to
timber hanger

The whole structure may be stiffened by the insertion of solid or herringbone strutting between the joists; this has another advantage – it also helps to prevent the joists from warping and distorting the floor surface. It will be covered with square-edged or tongued-and-grooved floorboards in older homes, or with sheets of flooring-grade chipboard in more modern ones.

Openings in the floor structure – round a stairwell, for example, or a chimney stack – are formed with doubled joists called trimming joists running parallel with the floor joists at either side of the opening. Trimmer joists are fixed at right angles to the trimming joists to form the other sides of the opening. The trimmer joists also support the cut (trimmed) ends of the floor joists adjoining the opening. The trimmer and trimmed joists are supported on joist hangers in modern homes and are fixed with cut timber joints in older buildings.

The ends of upper floor joists in the modern home are tied into the masonry with special restraint joist hangers at 2m intervals to give the external walls extra support. Joists running parallel with the walls are tied to them with transverse steel strapping, which usually extends over two or three joists.

THE TROUBLE WITH UPPER FLOORS

The only major problem likely to affect upper floors is sagging of the floor structure, caused either by overloading of inadequately sized joists or by alteration work involving the removal of supporting partitions. Excessive notching of joists during plumbing or wiring installation work can also lead to joists being weakened and sagging under a load. Minor damage to floorboards is usually the result of boards having been lifted for the installation of wiring and pipework.

What to do

It may be possible to strengthen a sagging floor structure by bolting new joists alongside the existing ones, or by installing a transverse support beam in the room below to support the centres of the affected joists. Both these jobs are best left to a specialist contractor. Minor repairs to floorboards are straightforward DIY jobs (see pages 84–87).

Lifting a floorboard

You may need to lift a floorboard in order to access pipes or cables beneath the floor for repairs.

Tools *Thin-bladed knife; drill and twist drill bits; jigsaw; bolster chisel; hammer; screwdriver. Also for tongue-and-groove boards: circular saw (or panel saw or flooring saw).*

Materials *50 or 75mm floorboard nails; 75mm No. 8 screws; pieces of timber about 40mm square and 100mm longer than the width of the boards.*

Before you start First find out whether the boards are tongue-and-groove or square edge by poking a thin-bladed knife between them. If they are square edge, the blade will pass right through.

Removing a square-edge board

Before lifting the board, you must cut across it at each end just before it meets a joist. Lines of nails indicate joist centres.

1 Drill a 10mm starting hole near the edge of the board you want to remove, and complete the cut across it with a jigsaw.

2 Starting at one end, prise out fixing nails by levering up the board with a bolster chisel.

3 Once you have loosened one or two sets of nails, push the handle of a hammer under the board as far from the loose end as possible, and try to prise the board up. This sends a shock wave along the whole length, loosening nails farther along, which you can then remove.

4 Push the hammer farther forward, and repeat the process, until the board is free.

How to remove tongues

On tongue-and-groove boards, the tongues on each side of the board must be removed. If adjoining boards are to be lifted, only the tongues at the outer edges of the group need cutting.

1 Adjust the depth of cut on a circular saw so that the blade just protrudes below the underside of the tongue. This will avoid pipes and cables. Since floorboards are usually 19mm thick, the underside of the tongue will be about 13mm below the surface. If you do not have a circular saw, use a panel or flooring saw. Cut at a shallow angle.

2 Place the blade between the boards, switch on the power, and move the saw along the length of board. With the tongues removed you should be able to see the joists between the boards. Remove as you would a square-edge board.

Replacing a damaged floorboard

Follow the instructions opposite to lift the damaged board. It is then a simple job to cut and fit a replacement.

Tools *Saw; hammer; perhaps a chisel; perhaps an electric drill and 2mm twist bit.*

Materials *Floorboards exactly the same thickness and width as the old ones – you may need to have these specially cut and planed at a timber yard; 50 or 75mm floorboard nails; perhaps scraps of hardboard or plywood and panel pins.*

Laying square-edge boards

Cut the timber to the same length as the old board. Fix the new boards to each joist with floorboard nails.

Tongue-and-groove boards

1 Cut the first board to length, and shave off its tongue with a chisel or plane.

2 Lay it in position, butting its former tongued edge to the grooved edge of an existing board.

3 If a second board is needed, cut it to length, lay it on the joists and tap it into place so that its tongue locates in the groove of the first new board. Continue with the other boards.

4 When you come to the final board, you will probably have to shave off its tongue, as you will not be able to manoeuvre it into place with the tongue attached.

5 Fix the boards to the joists with floorboard nails. You will be able to see the positions of the joists from the lines of nails in the existing floorboards.

6 If nails have to be driven in near the end of a board, first drill pilot holes smaller than the nails to avoid splitting the wood.

CURING LOOSE AND SQUEAKING BOARDS

A floorboard squeaks because it is not firmly held to its joist. When someone steps on it, it springs under the weight, rubbing against a neighbouring board. A squeak can be temporarily cured by dusting talc down the side of the board.

A board becomes loose when one or more of its fixing nails loses its grip due to vibration or the movement of the joist below. Prise out the nail if it is still there and refix the board with a screw big enough to fill the hole left by the nail. A 50mm No. 8 screw should be suitable.

The screw will hold the board securely in place, and as it goes exactly into the same hole as the nail there should be no danger of striking a cable or pipe.

Draughtproofing a timber ground floor

Draughty floors are often a problem in older properties, where floorboards have shrunk with age.

Smaller gaps can be filled with mastic applied via a sealant gun. If you intend to sand the boards, choose a sealant close to the desired colour, or one that will absorb stain when you apply it to the boards. Rot will not set in after you have sealed the gaps as long as air can move freely beneath the floor through airbricks.

Fill large gaps (wider than 6mm) with strips of softwood planed to a wedge section. Apply PVA adhesive to the long sides of the strips and tap into place with a mallet. Once set, use a power sander to smooth off any raised edges.

Replacing a floor with chipboard

If a floor is beyond repair, it can be replaced more cheaply with chipboard than with new floorboards.

Flooring-grade chipboard is sold in two thicknesses – 19 and 22mm. For joists up to 460mm apart, use 19mm board. Chipboard is heavy, so use the smallest sheets available unless you have someone to help you. You can use square-edge boards, but sheets with tongue-and-groove edges make a more stable floor, and edge joints do not need any support battens.

Lay boards flat in a pile inside the house as soon as they are delivered. At least 24 hours before you begin work, loose-lay them so they can adjust to the moisture content of the room.

Tools *Circular saw; panel saw or flooring saw; hammer; brush for applying adhesive; rag; pencil.*

Materials *Chipboard; No. 10 gauge annular ring nails – 55mm nails for 19mm sheets, 60mm for 22mm sheets; lengths of 50mm square timber; 75mm oval nails; PVA wood adhesive.*

1 Start by taking up enough of the old floorboards to give space for the first row of chipboard sheets.

2 If there is not enough space between skirting board and joist to push in the chipboard, the skirting board will have to be removed from the wall.

3 Lay the first sheet of chipboard in one corner of the room.

4 A gap of 10mm must be left around the edge of the room to allow the chipboard to expand in damp weather. If you have removed the skirting, you can see this easily; if not, then push the sheet of chipboard hard against the wall beneath the skirting board, draw a line where it meets the skirting and then pull it out by 10mm.

Square edge sheets

1 Lay square-edge sheets with the long edge parallel with the joists. They must be supported on every edge, so the long sides should rest on the centre of a joist, and the ends should rest on a nogging.

2 Make the nogging from a piece of 50mm square-section wood placed between the joists and fixed with 75mm oval nails driven down at an angle through the nogging and into the joist.

3 If the width of the sheet does not suit your joists, cut the sheet to fit. However, if this involves too much waste it may be a better idea to use tongue-and-groove sheets which are laid across the joists and so do not have to be cut to width.

4 Nail the sheets at 300mm intervals all the way round, putting the nails 10mm in from the edge. On intermediate joists put nails about 600mm apart.

Tongue-and-groove sheets

1 Position tongue-and-groove sheets with the long edge across the joists and nail them down. Drive four nails into each joist, one 10mm from each edge and the others at equal distances.

2 The sheet must be supported at the ends, so saw off any overhang close to the side of the joist.

Completing the job

• Coat the meeting edges of all boards with PVA wood adhesive, then push them firmly together. The adhesive will prevent the floor from squeaking. Wipe any glue from the surface with a damp cloth.
• When you come to the end of a row, cut the sheet to fit. Use the offcut to begin the next row so that the joins do not coincide.

Damp-proofing basements and cellars

Rooms below ground level are prone to damp. Some damp problems can be solved with DIY methods, but if the walls have been treated and they still weep, seek advice from a surveyor.

Treating slight damp

If the damp is slight, treat the walls with a bituminous waterproofing compound. After cleaning the surface, apply two coats following the manufacturer's instructions.

Dealing with damp in a concrete floor

Damp rising through a concrete basement floor indicates that there is no damp-proof membrane in the floor, or that it has failed. It is difficult to locate such failures.

1 If the damp is not severe, clean the surface and repair any cracks or potholes.

2 Dry the floor surface as much as possible, using a fan heater, for example.

3 Brush on three coats of moisture-curing polyurethane sealant, allowing each to become touch-dry before applying the next. No more than four hours should elapse between coats.

4 Scatter dry sand over the final coat of sealant while it is still damp. Leave for three days, then brush off excess sand. Lay a self-smoothing compound following the manufacturer's instructions.

Staircases

The staircase is a major decorative feature and can make a lasting impression on potential buyers.

Apart from its aesthetic appeal, the most important feature of staircase design and construction is safety. The current Building Regulations have precise requirements for the steepness of a domestic staircase, the number and size of its treads and risers, the layout of landings and, most importantly, the provision of handrails and guarding on landings and alongside the flight. However, many millions of homes were built before these modern standards were introduced.

Staircase construction

The way a staircase is built has changed little over the centuries. However, mass production has led today to standardisation of sizes and dimensions, and anything out of the ordinary must still be hand-built.

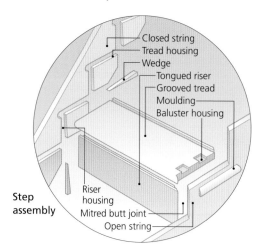

Closed string
Tread housing
Wedge
Tongued riser
Grooved tread
Moulding
Baluster housing
Riser housing
Mitred butt joint
Open string

Step assembly

Treads and risers The horizontal treads and vertical risers that form each step are supported in grooves in the strings, and are held in place by glued wedges. The short riser wedges are fitted first and are trimmed off flush with the underside of the tread below. The longer tread wedge locks the riser wedge in place when it is driven into its groove.

The treads and risers are tongued-and-grooved together on a traditional staircase. Pairs of triangular blocks are glued into the internal angles between each tread and the riser below it. On modern stairs the treads and risers may be butt-jointed, again with blocks in the internal angles.

The risers are absent on open-plan staircases, and the strings are often linked with steel rods beneath the treads for extra stability. Alternatively, there may be a central bearer (carriage) running the length of the staircase to support the treads.

Strings A typical staircase consists of two angled side timbers, called strings, fixed between the two floor levels that the stairs connect. Where the staircase has one open side, the string at that side may be cut into steps along its top edge. The outer ends of the treads rest on these steps, instead of being housed in grooves in the sides of the string. This is called an open string; the other (uncut) string is a closed string.

Handrail construction A staircase rising between two walls needs no guarding but, for safety's sake, a handrail is often fixed to one or both walls – either direct to the masonry, or mounted on wall brackets. On other staircases, a stout newel post is fitted at the top and bottom of the flight. These are bolted to the floor joists at each end of the flight, or bedded in the floor screed and secured with a metal dowel if the ground floor is solid. Original newel posts will be a single component, but replacements are dowel-jointed into a stub of the original. The ends of the outer string are tenoned into mortises cut in the posts. Additional posts are installed wherever the staircase changes direction – at a quarter or half landing. They are often topped with decorative knobs, or finials.

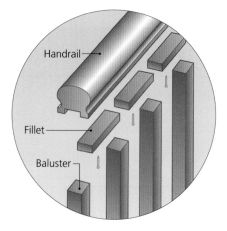

Handrail
Fillet
Baluster

Handrail A handrail is fitted between the newel posts, just below their tops, using special angled brackets to form the primary guarding on the staircase and, if required, round the landing.

Balusters The space between the handrail and the staircase string is filled with evenly spaced vertical balusters, horizontal rails, wrought iron panels, safety glass or solid panelling. This secondary guarding is there to stop someone using the stairs from falling between the handrail and the string. If balusters are used, their top ends are nailed into a channel machined in the underside of the handrail.

On a closed-string staircase, the bottom ends fit into the groove in a continuous base rail fixed to the top edge of the string. Small spacing fillets of wood are fitted between the balusters under the handrail and on the base rail. On an open-string staircase, the bottom ends of the balusters fit into notches cut in the treads, and are retained there by mouldings pinned and glued to the tread ends.

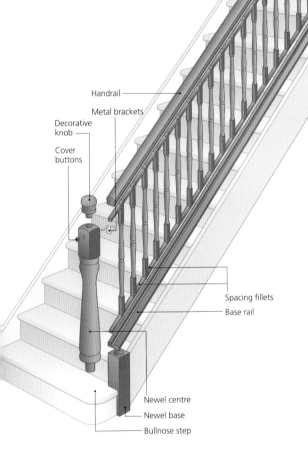

Turned balusters

Handrail

Metal brackets

Decorative knob

Cover buttons

Spacing fillets

Base rail

Newel centre

Newel base

Bullnose step

Bullnose step The lowest step (sometimes two steps) of the flight may project beyond the bottom newel post, and their open ends have a characteristic rounded shape. They are known as bullnose steps.

THE TROUBLE WITH STAIRCASES

General wear and tear on staircases results in creaking treads and split or cracked tread nosings (the front edge that overhangs the riser below). There is obviously a potential safety risk if the balustrade is loose, or if any components are broken.

Shrinkage and settlement can result in the closed string of the staircase pulling away from the wall next to the flight. Loose or failed fixings can result in joints opening up anywhere on the flight.

Insect attack can be a problem, especially in understairs cupboards where exposed rough wood provides a perfect site for wood-boring insects such as woodworm to lay their eggs. The tell-tale exit holes left in the wood by the emerging beetles are a sure sign of an infestation.

What to do
You can carry out minor repairs to the staircase and its balustrade yourself (see pages 90–91). Call in a professional to tackle major repairs. Woodworm can be tackled with DIY treatments, since the affected area is relatively small and self-contained.

Fixing creaking stairs

Stairs creak when a tread or riser is not securely fixed and rubs against an adjacent piece of wood. The cure is straightforward if the underside of the staircase is accessible.

Working from underneath

Once you have determined which tread is creaking, the best remedy is to add extra wood angle blocks, screwed and glued to the tread and riser from underneath.

Tools *Saw; bradawl; drill and twist bits; screwdriver.*

Materials *Blocks of wood about 40mm triangular or square in section and about 75mm long; PVA adhesive; four No. 8 screws per block (choose a length that will not break through the face of the stair).*

1 Drill four clearance holes in each block – one pair at right angles to the other.

2 Apply PVA adhesive to the blocks and push them in place.

3 Secure the blocks to the tread and riser with four screws.

4 If possible, strengthen the join between the riser and the tread below by squeezing PVA adhesive into the join. Then drive three evenly spaced screws horizontally through the riser and into the tread. Position the screws 12mm up from the bottom of the riser.

Working from above

You will have to lift the stair carpet to work on the treads. Try brushing some talcum powder into the squeaking join to act as a lubricant. If the squeak continues, screw down the front of the tread onto the riser.

Tools *Old chisel; drill and twist bits; countersink bit; screwdriver; filling knife; abrasive paper.*

Materials *PVA adhesive; 38mm No. 8 countersunk screws; filler.*

1 Using a chisel, force apart the top of the riser and the tread above, and insert some glue in the space: this is only possible if the treads and risers are not jointed together.

2 Drill clearance holes every 250mm through the tread and pilot holes into the top of the riser. Countersink the clearance holes so screws will sit below surface level. Insert the screws and screw down tight.

3 Cover screw heads with filler and smooth with abrasive paper. If the stairs are varnished, use a matching wood filler.

Repairing broken balusters

If you have all the pieces, it may be possible to mend a damaged baluster; if not, you will have to replace it.

Tools *Mallet; old chisel; handsaw; hammer; vice clamp.*

Materials *New baluster if needed; nails (same length as the old ones).*

Before you start If the baluster has split or a piece has broken off, apply PVA adhesive to the two surfaces and bind them with insulating tape. Clamp the baluster between two blocks of wood until the adhesive has dried. Then remove the tape and smooth off any hardened adhesive with fine abrasive paper.

Square section balusters are easy to match, but you may have to pay a wood turner to reproduce a fancy one for you.

1 Free the baluster at the bottom. If the outer string is open prise off the cover moulding on the side of the tread. Then gently tap the bottom end of the baluster out of its slot with a mallet.

If the outer string is 'closed' (its top and bottom edges are parallel and the tread and riser slot into grooves), a baluster on an old staircase may be held in a mortise or it may be pinned. Scrape away the paint to check. If it is mortised use a handsaw to cut through it at the bottom following the line of the string. If it is pinned, knock it out with the mallet.

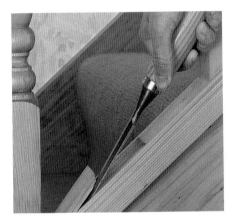

Alternatively On a modern staircase it may be held at the bottom between fillets of wood. Lift out the broken baluster, and lever out the lower fillet.

2 Remove the top part of the broken baluster by tapping it with a mallet so it is freed from the rail. If there is no space between the balusters to wield the mallet, place the end of a piece of wood against the baluster and tap the other end with the mallet. Or pull out the baluster by hand.

3 Use the broken baluster as a pattern to mark the correct slope on the top of the new one. Before you cut it to length, make sure that you have got the measurement right.

4 Hold the new baluster in a vice and cut along the marked line.

FIXING LOOSE BALUSTERS

Balusters are usually fixed to the handrail by nails driven through them at an angle, and into the underside of the rail. Sometimes they are fitted between fillets of wood.

Nailing the baluster If a nail works loose, try to remove it with pincers, and insert a longer, slightly thicker nail in its place. If you can't remove it, drive another one in at a different place. On slender balusters drill a fine pilot hole first. Do not use glue. The baluster may have to be removed at some time in the future.

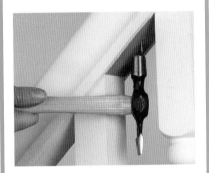

Replacing a fillet The balusters must be fitted into a groove in the underside of the rail, with the spaces between balusters filled with fillets of wood. If a fillet has dropped out, cut a new piece of wood to the right size and nail it in place.

5 Fit an open (cut) string back in place in its notch on the tread and nail the baluster to the handrail at the top. On a closed string, use the old baluster to cut the angle at the bottom and fit the new one in place, top and bottom. If the baluster was mortised into the string, it will have to be nailed in place.

Doors

Whether internal or external, pay attention to the fit of a door in its frame to make sure that it opens and closes freely. Poorly fitting external doors can let in draughts and rain in bad weather.

External door frames

The timber frame for an external door is prefabricated, and consists of a sill, two side members called jambs and a door head. The components are jointed with mortise-and-tenon joints or held together with steel dowels. The sill is usually made from hardwood for durability, and projects from the frame like a window sill to throw rainwater clear of the wall below.

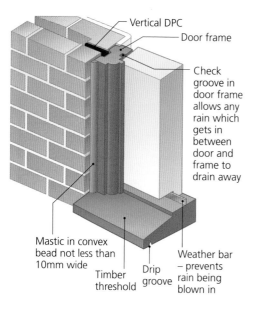

Vertical DPC
Door frame
Check groove in door frame allows any rain which gets in between door and frame to drain away
Mastic in convex bead not less than 10mm wide
Timber threshold
Drip groove
Weather bar – prevents rain being blown in

The door sill has grooves machined in its underside. The outermost is the drip groove which stops water from running back under the sill, while the inner one helps to fix the frame on its mortar bed when it is set in place in the wall just above the level of the house damp-proof course. A plastic or metal strip called a weather bar is set in a groove in the upper surface of the sill. This stops water from blowing under the door when it is closed.

The sides and head of the frame are rebated, allowing the door to close securely against the frame. This rebate also contains a drip groove or integral weatherstripping.

Aluminium and steel-framed plastic (uPVC) door frames are made up in a similar way from specially-formed cross sections, and usually incorporate weatherstripping as part of the design.

The frame of an external door is set in place before the walls are built up around it, and is tied into the masonry with galvanised steel ties screwed to the frame and bedded into the mortar courses.

Internal door frames

Internal doors usually have simple three-sided timber frames, made from two jambs and a door head. The frame is commonly referred to as a door lining. In older houses it may be rebated like an external frame, but in modern houses it is usually formed from plain timber. Slim timber battens called stop beads are pinned to the door lining after installation to form a rebate against which the door closes.

In a masonry wall The lining is fixed direct to the masonry – probably with large cut nails in older properties, and with screws and wallplugs or nailable frame fixings in a modern house. The timber used is usually about 25mm wider than the wall thickness, creating an edge against which the wall plaster can be finished. This joint is covered with architrave mouldings pinned to the edges of the door lining once plastering is complete.

In thin (75mm) blockwork partitions, the sides of the frame may extend from floor to ceiling, with the door head fixed between them and the space above it filled with blockwork. This type of storey-height frame is stronger than one built into an opening with a lintel over it.

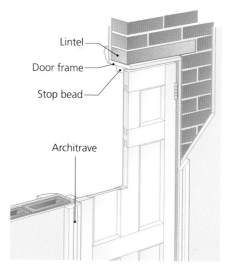

Lintel
Door frame
Stop bead
Architrave

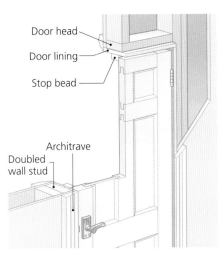

Door head
Door lining
Stop bead
Architrave
Doubled wall stud

In timber-framed partition walls Vertical studs form the sides of the opening and the door head is nailed between them. Sometimes thicker studs are used here, or double studs are fitted for extra strength and rigidity. A thin door lining is nailed within the opening, providing an edge to which the plasterboard cladding on the partition can be abutted.

Again, architrave mouldings cover the join and stop beads form a rebate against which the door closes.

Safe glazing

Part N of the Building Regulations lays down strict rules about the use of glass in and next to doors. Briefly, glass panels in all doors and in fixed panes beside door openings should be of toughened glass marked 'Made to British Standard BS6206 Class A'. This requirement also applies to any double-glazed panels.

THE TROUBLE WITH DOORS

Rot is the main enemy of external doors and their frames if they are not kept in good decorative order, or if the sealant between frame and masonry fails. Internal and external doors can suffer from warping or binding in their frames, and may be affected by worn or damaged hinges. Most minor faults can be repaired by a competent do-it-yourselfer (see pages 93–97).

Replacing a door requires moderate carpentry skills and you may prefer to leave the job to a carpenter.

Curing faults in doors

Most faults in doors can be cured quite easily. For some jobs you may need another person to help you, or to steady the door while you work on it.

Door binding along one side

Doors often bind (stick) in their frames because regular repainting causes a build-up of paint on the edge of the door and on the frame.

1 Strip off the paint. Do this mechanically to avoid damaging the finish on the door faces. Use either a power sander or a Surform planer file.

2 Smooth the stripped surfaces with glasspaper and check that the door opens and closes easily.

3 There should be a slight gap between the edge of the door and the frame. To check for this, run a thin knife blade all round the edge of the door when it is closed. Where the gap is insufficient, strip and then plane that edge of the door. You may have to take the door off its hinges, and perhaps remove locks and latches.

4 Prime and paint the stripped edges of the door. Then let the paint dry before closing the door.

Door binding at the bottom

If an external door binds at its lower corners, the problem is often caused by moisture being absorbed through an unpainted bottom edge.

1 Take the door off its hinges and dry the bare wood thoroughly with a hot-air gun.

2 Seal the bare edge with two coats of quick-drying wood primer. Re-hang the door when the primer is touch-dry. Painting is unnecessary as the edge is out of sight.

3 If the binding is severe, hold the door on one of its long edges in a portable workbench. Mark a line to work to, then plane downwards from the edges of the door to the centre; this will avoid splintering the edge.

4 Prime the bare edge as in step 2 and re-hang the door.

Door binding at the top

You may be able to plane the top edge of a door (which is often unpainted) without taking it off its hinges. Prop it open with wedges while you work from a stepladder. Otherwise take it off its hinges and plane the whole edge as in step 3 above.

Door squeaks

Oil the hinge pins with an aerosol lubricant. Work the door backwards and forwards a few times to get the lubricant into the hinge, then wipe away any surplus with kitchen roll.

With rising butt hinges, lift the open door off the hinge pins and lightly smear them with grease or petroleum jelly. Wipe away the surplus after re-hanging the door.

Door tends to slam

The best solution for a slamming door is to fit a door closer, which slows down the speed at which the door shuts.

1 A template is always supplied with a door closer. Decide whether you want the door to open to 100° (straight into the room) or 180° (flat back to the hinge wall), and use a bradawl or a pencil to mark through the appropriate template spots.

2 Drill pilot holes and screw the door closer onto the door.

3 With the door closer fitted to the door, you can now mark the position of the pivot arm on the door architrave. Chisel out a recess and screw it in position.

4 Fix the pivot arm to the body of the closer and turn the adjusting screws so that the door shuts smoothly and slowly without slamming.

Door panels split

Sometimes splits develop in the panels of old doors. The solution depends on whether the door is painted or varnished.

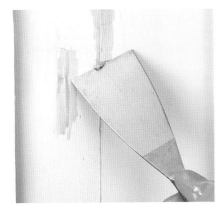

Painted door

On a painted door, fill the crack with a wood filler and paint over it.

Natural wood door

On a varnished door where the filler will show, drive dowels into the edge of the door to press against the edges of the panel and close the crack.

1 First clean out old varnish or filler from the crack with a sharp knife.

2 Drill two or three 8mm diameter holes through the edge of the door to line up with the near edge of the panel. Measure the thickness of the door stile and mark the drill bit with a piece of tape to act as a depth stop.

3 Cut some 8mm dowels about 20mm longer than the width of the stiles.

4 Squirt PVA wood adhesive into the crack in the panel and into the holes in the stile. Drive the dowels into the holes.

5 Wipe off excess adhesive with a damp cloth. Leave the protruding dowel until the glue has set, then trim it off flush with the door edge. Sand the cut end smooth.

Lock stiff to turn

1 Spray aerosol lubricant into a surface-mounted lock using the applicator tube provided. Squirt the lubricant through the latch and bolt holes and through the keyhole.

2 If this is not sufficient, remove the lock from the door, take off one side of the case, and lightly grease the mechanism. Before starting work, note the positions of the components so they can be put back if they become displaced.

Do not use oil or aerosol lubricants in Yale-type cylinder locks; they attract grit. Instead puff graphite powder or PTFE dry powder lubricant into the keyhole.

Latch will not engage

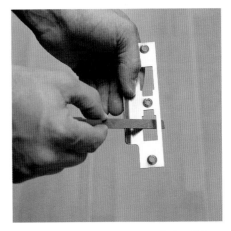

If a door sags a little, the latch bolt will be out of alignment with the striking plate. You can correct a small misalignment by unscrewing the plate and enlarging its cut-out with a small metal file.

Otherwise, remove the striking plate and re-fix it a little lower down the frame. Use a sharp chisel and a mallet to extend the recess in which it fits. If the plate has to be moved only a small distance, drill out the old screw holes and fill them with dowels. Drill new pilot holes for the fixing screws.

Door frame loose

For a loose door frame make new fixings with three frame plugs at each side of the frame (see next page). The length of the frame plugs, which come complete with hammer-in screws, should be the thickness of the frame plus at least 60mm.

1 Using a masonry bit, drill through the frame and into the wall behind it to the required depth.

2 Hammer the screw and plug into the hole until the head is flush with the frame.

Door hard to close

A door that is difficult to close, and tends to spring open, is said to be hinge-bound. The problem is usually caused by hinge recesses cut too deep in either the door edge or in the frame. Hinge flaps should be flush with the surface of the wood.

1 Open the door fully and then put a wedge under it.

2 Clear any paint from the slots in the hinge screws, and remove the screws.

3 Get someone to steady the door while you lever the hinge flap out of its recess. Pack out the recess with one or more pieces of cardboard until the hinge is flush with the wood surface, then replace the screws. Use new screws if you damaged the slots of the old ones.

Protruding screw heads
Hinges may bind because the screws have been put in askew, or because their heads are too large to fit flush in the countersinks in the hinge flaps.

Remove the offending screws and replace them with screws with smaller heads. If they will not tighten, pack out the holes with glued-in matches.

Alternatively Deepen the countersinks in the hinge flaps so that the screw heads will be flush with the surface. Use a high-speed-steel countersink bit.

If the screws were originally set in askew, drill out and plug the old screw holes with dowels and drill new pilot holes for the screws.

Badly placed hinge flaps
Binding can also be caused by hinge flaps that are set into the frame too near to the door stop. As the door is closed, the face of the door presses against the stop.

1 Remove the hinges, drill out the old screw holes and plug them with glued dowels. Chisel the dowel ends off flush with the recess.

2 Drill new fixing holes so that the hinge is farther away from the door stop. The hinge pin should be just clear of the door edge. Fill the resulting gaps beside the repositioned hinges with wood filler.

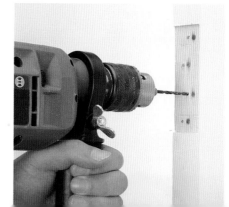

Alternatively On an internal door, it may be easier to prise off and reposition the door stop, which is usually a separate piece of wood pinned to the door frame.

Door is rotting

If exterior doors have not been protected with paint or varnish, rot may set in, especially near the bottom and at joints. You can repair minor damage with wood hardener and high-performance exterior wood filler.

1 Chisel away the rotten wood and use a hot-air gun to dry the exposed bare wood.

2 Treat the area with the wood hardener. When this has soaked in and dried, fill the recess with the filler. Build it up slightly above the surface, and sand it flat when it has hardened.

3 Repaint the door to disguise the repair.

Frame is rotting

External door frames often rot near the sill. The only satisfactory repair is to insert a new piece of timber. Use an all-purpose saw; the teeth will not be blunted by accidental contact with masonry.

1 Probe the wood with a sharp knife to reveal where the soft, rotten section ends. Make a 45° downward cut into the frame about 75mm above this point.

2 Prise the rotten part away from the wall.

3 Cut a length of new wood to fit the gap, sloping one end to align with the saw cut. Test its fit and adjust it as necessary. The old frame may have a door stop machined into it. Make a matching section from two or more pieces of wood glued and cramped together.

4 When the new section is a good fit, treat all its surfaces with clear wood preservative. Drill and countersink holes in it, and mark the fixing positions on the wall through these holes. Drill and plug the wall and screw the section in place.

5 Where the old and new frame section join, drill 8mm holes through the joint at right angles to it. Smear glue on 8mm hardwood dowels and hammer them into the holes.

6 Trim the dowels flush with the surface when the glue has dried. Prime and paint.

Door sags

When the bottom corner of the door rubs on the floor, the cause is either faulty hinges or loose joints in the door. Partly open the door and lift the handle to see if there is movement at the hinges or joints.

Faulty hinges
If the hinge screws are loose, try tightening them. If they will not hold, remove them, drill out the screw holes and plug them with glued dowels. Drill new pilot holes and refit the screws.

If the movement is in the knuckle of the hinge due to a worn hinge pin, the only cure is to fit new hinges. The hinges may not be large enough to support the weight of the door. In this case fit larger, stronger hinges, and add a third hinge midway between them if you are working on a front door.

Loose door joints
If corner joints on a framed door are loose, glue and cramp them back into place.

1 Take the door off its hinges, and try to prise the loose joints apart.

2 Squirt wood adhesive into the joints and cramp them closed with sash cramps. Be sure to check that the door frame is square.

3 On the edge of the door, drive small wooden wedges into the ends of the tenons in order to prevent the joints from opening up again.

4 Drill through the face of the door and the tenon, and drive a glued dowel into the hole to lock the tenon in place. Trim off the dowels flush with the surface of the door.

Fireplaces, flues and chimneys

Central heating has made the fireplace almost redundant in modern homes, although consumer demand means that one is still often provided in the main living room.

In older homes there was a fireplace in every room, and the construction of the flues that were needed to discharge the smoke was the most complex part of the whole house structure.

In terraced houses, the flues were built into the party walls between the properties. In larger houses, there would often be two or more chimney stacks, each containing two or four flues and serving downstairs and upstairs fireplaces, plus a separate chimney for the coal-fired boiler that heated the house's hot water supply.

Fireplaces

The simplest type of fireplace, found in old and unmodernised homes, is just a brick opening at the base of the flue. A free-standing grate is set on a concrete hearth, and the fire is built within the grate. As it burns, the hot gases it creates rise into the flue and draw fresh air in from the room through the base of the grate to keep the fire burning.

This arrangement is very wasteful of heat, and often suffers from smoke blowing back into the room. Birds also have a habit of falling down the open flue.

Firebacks

Most fireplaces have a shaped fireback built into the basic brick recess. This is a shaped fireclay unit, available in several pieces that are bonded together with fire cement at assembly. The fireback helps to retain the heat of the fire, reflecting it back into the room. The void between the fireback and the brick recess is usually filled with a mixture of sand, lime and broken brick (or simply builder's rubble) in older homes, or with lightweight insulating concrete in newer ones.

Flues

The fireplace is linked to the open flue above it with a sloping connector called a throat. This was formed from mortar in older homes, but in modern chimneys a pre-cast concrete throat unit is built in as the chimney is constructed. The joints between the fireback and the throat are sealed with fireproof rope. This also seals the joint between the fireback and a decorative fire surround fitted round the fireplace opening.

The concrete hearth is often topped with a decorative 'superimposed' hearth of ceramic or quarry tiles or stone slabs.

Chimney construction

Modern chimneys are lined with special interlocking clay flue blocks, which allow for a smooth upward flow of smoke and prevent soot and tar from collecting. Such deposits are in any case less of a problem today, thanks to the widespread use of processed fuels rather than raw coal.

The chimney stack projects above the roof line so that down-draughts do not affect the upwards draw of the flue. Each flue within the chimney is topped by a chimney pot, which is set on a mortar bed and secured by a shaped cap of mortar called flaunching round its base. If the flue has become disused, the pots may have been removed and replaced by a cowl or a cover slab. The latter is likely to be found where the fireplaces have themselves been decommissioned and blocked up.

THE TROUBLE WITH CHIMNEYS

Indoors, the main problem with chimneys, especially disused ones, is tar and soot staining being carried through to the inner face of the flue by condensation occurring within it. Externally, the exposed part of the chimney stack can suffer from failed pointing and flaunching, loose chimney pots, damage to the brickwork and to the flashings that weatherproof the junction between the stack and the roof slope.

What to do

Make sure that disused flues are properly capped off and have adequate ventilation at top and bottom. Inspect the chimney stack regularly so that faults can be spotted and rectified before they become serious. Unless you are experienced in working at heights, it is best to leave chimney stack repairs to a professional builder.

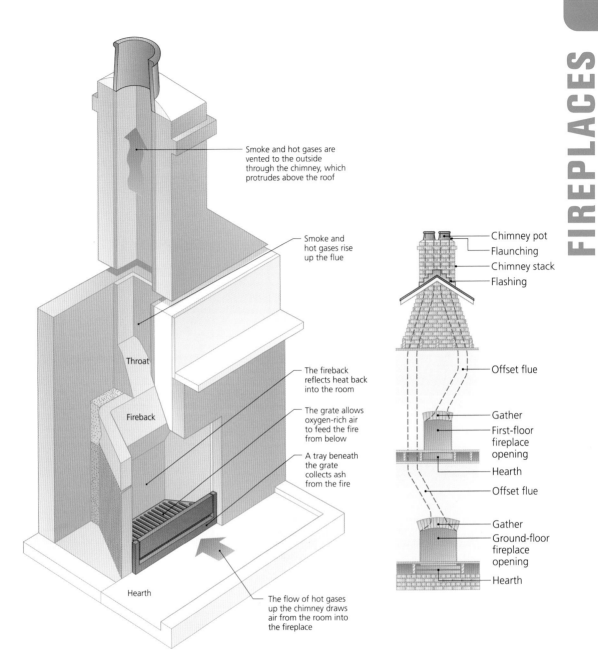

Smoke and hot gases are vented to the outside through the chimney, which protrudes above the roof

Smoke and hot gases rise up the flue

Throat

The fireback reflects heat back into the room

Fireback

The grate allows oxygen-rich air to feed the fire from below

A tray beneath the grate collects ash from the fire

Hearth

The flow of hot gases up the chimney draws air from the room into the fireplace

Chimney pot
Flaunching
Chimney stack
Flashing

Offset flue

Gather
First-floor fireplace opening

Hearth

Offset flue

Gather
Ground-floor fireplace opening

Hearth

The traditional chimney is a hollow brick column with an open hearth or fireplace at the bottom and a chimney pot at the top. Generally speaking, the higher the chimney is, the more efficient it is at drawing smoke and fumes up and away. The chimney may be free-standing (especially in a timber-framed house), but is usually built into an external or internal wall for support. On an external wall, the flue may be built on the inside of the wall or on the outside. An inside flue creates a projecting chimney breast flanked by two alcoves within the room, whereas an outside flue leaves the fireplace opening flush with the wall surface. The chimney is straight if it has a single flue. If it contains multiple flues, each is offset so that the downstairs flue by-passes the upstairs fireplace.

Old flues were unlined, or were rendered internally with mortar, which cracked and failed as time went by. Condensation within the flue could eventually carry tar and soot stains through the unprotected masonry to ruin room decorations. Soot would accumulate within the flue, often leading to messy soot falls and eventually to chimney fires.

Making good

Minor damage is part of the wear and tear of living in a house. Woodwork can be dented or split. Plaster can crack or come away from the surface beneath. Gaps can open up where skirting boards and architraves meet the wall. When it is time to redecorate, all these defects can be made good very simply, using the appropriate filler or sealant and the right tools. The basic techniques for repairing woodwork are described here; for repairs to plaster see pages 75–77.

Choosing fillers

There is a daunting array of fillers available in DIY stores, ranging from traditional dry powder that you mix with water, to ready-mixed products in tubes, tubs, tins and cartridges. Powder fillers can be kept for a long time if they are stored in dry conditions, but ready-mixed fillers have a finite shelf life. Buy them only if you have a lot of filling to do in a short space of time, and are likely to use up most of the filler.

You need three basic types of filler for everyday DIY – a filler for wood, a filler for plaster and a filler for gaps. So-called 'all-purpose' fillers are available, but as with all products of this type their performance is a compromise. They will fill anything adequately, but you will get better results with a one-job filler designed specifically for its purpose.

Repairing woodwork

Existing woodwork, whether painted or varnished, can become dented or chipped from everyday wear and tear. These defects need filling before the surface is given a new finish. Use interior wood filler on woodwork that will be painted, and wood stopper in a matching wood shade for woodwork that will be varnished.

There are also two-part products for really tough filling jobs. They consist of a basic filler and a chemical hardening agent. You add a small amount of the hardening agent to activate the ingredients of the

filler, to start the setting process. This type of filler is particularly good for repairing damage caused by rot.

1 Sand the damaged area with fine wet-and-dry abrasive paper. This will smooth any rough edges to the damage, and will key the surface so that the filler will bond better to it. Wipe away any dust with kitchen roll moistened with white spirit.

2 Use your filling knife to press wood filler or stopper into the damage, leaving it a little proud of the surrounding surface. Leave it to set hard.

3 Sand the filled area smooth with fine abrasive paper, then wipe away dust with kitchen roll as in step 1. The repair is now ready for redecorating.

Using wood filler

The type of wood filler you choose depends on whether the wood is going to be painted or simply waxed or varnished.

Wood must have a well-prepared surface before the final finish is applied. This means filling any holes before the wood is finally sanded smooth. If the wood is to be left its natural colour, buy a wood filler that matches. If it is going to be painted, fill with an interior filler.

Tools *Filling knife; abrasive paper; electric sander.*

Materials *Interior filler or wood filler.*

1 If you plan to paint the wood, use a power sander with fine abrasive paper to key existing paintwork. Then wash it with a solution of hot water and sugar soap.

2 If you are repainting the area, use interior wood filler to fill any defects such as cracks or dents. Be sure to press the filler in firmly and scrape away any excess.

3 Once the filler has set hard, sand it smooth ready for painting.

4 If you intend to apply a finish through which the wood can be seen – stain, wax or varnish – then sand it smooth and fill it with a wood filler (known as stopping) that matches the colour of the bare wood as closely as possible.

5 Press the stopping into the holes and cracks, taking care not to spread it into the surrounding grain.

6 Wait until the stopping has dried to the same colour all over – usually about 30 minutes – then sand it flat.

Filling open woodgrain

If a wooden door has a very open grain, and you want to achieve a smooth painted finish, you will need to work in a paste of fine-surface filler. Apply the filler with a flexible filling knife, pushing it right into the grain. Then wipe away the excess with a damp rag.

Repairing a dripping tap

A dripping tap usually means that the tap washer needs renewing, but can also be caused by a damaged valve seating. If the drip is from a mixer spout, renew both tap washers.

Tools *One large open-ended spanner, normally 20mm for a 12mm tap or 24mm for a 19mm tap (or use an adjustable spanner); old screwdriver (for prising). Possibly also one small spanner (normally 8mm); one or two pipe wrenches; cloth for padding jaws; one 5mm, one 10mm screwdriver.*

Materials *Replacement washer or a washer-and-jumper valve unit; alternatively, a washer-and-seating set; petroleum jelly. Possibly also penetrating oil.*

Removing the headgear

1 Cut off the water supply. Make sure the tap is turned fully on, and put the plug into the plughole to stop any small parts falling down the waste pipe.

2 Unscrew or lever off the cover of a non-rising spindle tap to expose the retaining screw. Remove the screw and put it in a safe place. Remove the head.

Alternatively With a rising spindle tap, prise off the index disc and remove the retaining screw to release the capstan from the

Rising spindle tap The jumper valve is in the shape of a rod and plate, and the washer is attached to the base of the plate. When changing a washer, the handle is lifted off with the headgear. When adjusting the gland nut, the handle has to be removed so that the bell-shaped cover can be pulled off out of the way.

Non-rising spindle tap The jumper valve and washer are the same as in a traditional rising spindle tap, but the spindle is sealed by an O-ring nut rather than a gland nut. The tap handle and headgear have to be removed to change a washer or to renew an O-ring.

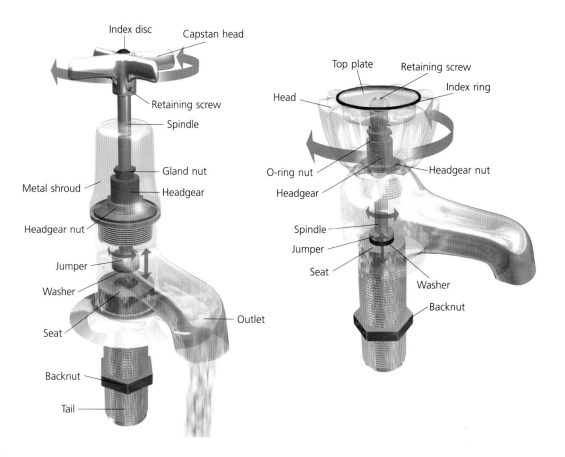

spindle. Use a wrench wrapped in cloth to unscrew the metal shroud and lift it away from the headgear nut.

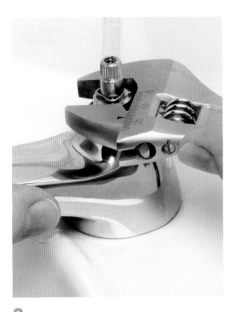

3 Undo the headgear nut with a spanner. Do not force the nut, if it is stiff. Brace the tap body by hand or with a pipe wrench wrapped in a cloth, to prevent the tap from turning and fracturing the pipework attached to it.

4 If the nut is still difficult to turn, apply penetrating oil round the joint, wait about ten minutes to give it time to soak in, then try again. You may have to make several applications.

Fitting the washer

1 Prise off the washer with a screwdriver. If there is a small nut holding it in place, unscrew it with a spanner (normally 8mm). If it is difficult to undo, put penetrating oil round it and try again when it has soaked in. Then prise off the washer.

Alternatively If the nut is impossible to remove, you can replace both the jumper valve and washer in one unit.

2 After fitting a new washer or washer and jumper, grease the threads on the base of the tap before reassembling.

Repairing the valve seating

Washer-and-jumper valve unit

Plastic seating

Valve seat

When renewing a washer, inspect the valve seat inside the tap body. If it is scaled or scored by grit, the seal between washer and seat will not be effective even with a new washer.

The simplest repair is with a washer-and-seating set. This has a plastic seat to fit into the valve seat, and a washer-and-jumper valve unit to fit into the headgear.

When the tap is turned off, the plastic seating is forced firmly into place. It may take a few days for the new seating to give a completely watertight fit.

An alternative repair is to buy or hire a tap reseating tool and grind the seat smooth yourself.

Tap conversion kit

You may be able to buy a tap conversion kit to change the style of taps and replace worn or broken mechanisms. Newer heads can be changed back to Victorian brass heads, or a tap with a crutch or capstan handle can be given a newer look. The spout and body of the tap remain in place.

Some kits have bushes to fit different tap sizes. The kits are available from most DIY stores and fitting instructions are included.

Cleaning or replacing ceramic discs

Ceramic disc taps operate on a different principle from conventional taps that have washers and spindles. Positioned in the body of the tap is a cartridge containing a pair of ceramic discs, each with two holes in it.

One disc is fixed in position; the other rotates when the handle is turned. As the movable disc rotates, the holes in it line up with the holes in the fixed one and water flows through them. When the tap is turned off the movable disc rotates so that the holes no longer align.

Dealing with a dripping tap

If a scratched ceramic disc is causing the leak, the entire cartridge must be replaced: left-handed for a hot tap or right-handed for a cold tap. Remove the old cartridge and take it with you when buying a replacement to make sure it is the correct size and 'hand'. Ceramic taps can also drip at the base of the cartridge if the seal has perished. Replace it if necessary.

Checking discs in a ceramic disc mixer tap

1 Turn off the water supply. Pull off the tap handles (it may be necessary to unscrew a small retaining screw on each) and use a spanner to unscrew the headgear section.

2 Carefully remove the ceramic cartridges, keeping hot and cold separate. Check both cartridges for dirt and wear and tear.

3 If the cartridges are worn, replace with identical parts for the tap unit. Make sure the hot and cold cartridges are fitted into the correct taps.

4 If the cartridges are dirty, clean them with a damp cloth. Replace the rubber seal, if it is worn. Replace the cartridge in the tap unit, fitting the hot and cold cartridges into the appropriate taps.

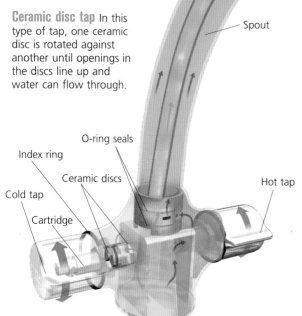

Ceramic disc tap In this type of tap, one ceramic disc is rotated against another until openings in the discs line up and water can flow through.

Spout

Index ring

O-ring seals

Ceramic discs

Cold tap

Cartridge

Hot tap

AVOIDING HARD-WATER DAMAGE TO TAPS

If you live in a hard-water area, you should check your taps for damage, once a year.

Turn off the mains water supply. One at a time check that the headgear on each tap unscrews easily. Use penetrating oil to release stiff nuts and use a spanner and a wrench wrapped in a cloth to hold the body of the tap as you turn.

If limescale has built up, remove and soak small parts in vinegar or limescale remover. Smear the thread with lubricant before reassembling.

Curing a leak from a spindle or spout

Leakage from the body of the tap – from round the spindle, the base of a swivel spout, or the diverter knob on a shower mixer tap – may indicate a faulty gland or O-ring seal.

Possible causes This sort of leak is most likely to occur on a kitchen cold tap with a bell-shaped cover and visible spindle. Soapy water from wet hands may have run down the spindle and washed the grease out of the gland that makes a watertight joint round the spindle. If the tap is sometimes used with a hosepipe, back pressure from the hose connection will also weaken the gland.

On a modern tap, especially one with a shrouded head, there is an O-ring seal instead of a gland, and it rarely needs replacing. However, an O-ring seal may occasionally become worn.

Tools *Small spanner (normally 12mm) or adjustable spanner. Possibly also one 5mm and one 10mm screwdriver; penknife or screwdriver for prising; two small wooden blocks about 10mm deep (such as spring clothes pegs).*

Materials *Packing materials (gland-packing string or PTFE tape). Possibly also silicone grease; O-rings (and possibly washers) of the correct size – take the old ones with you when buying, or give the make of tap.*

Adjusting the gland

There is no need to cut off the water supply to the tap.

1 With the tap turned off, undo the small screw that secures the capstan handle and put it in a safe place (it is very easily lost), then remove the handle. If there is no screw, the handle should pull off.

2 Remove the bell-shaped cover to reveal the gland nut – the highest nut on the spindle. Tighten the nut about half a turn with a spanner.

3 Turn the tap on by temporarily slipping the handle back on, then check whether there is still a leak from the spindle. If there is not, turn the gland nut another quarter turn and reassemble the tap. Do not overtighten the gland nut, or the tap will be hard to turn off.

4 If there is still a leak, give another half turn and check again.

5 If the gland continues leaking after you have adjusted it as far as possible, repack the gland.

Replacing the packing

1 With the tap turned off and the handle and cover removed, use a spanner to remove the gland nut and lift it out.

2 Pick out the old packing with a small screwdriver. Replace it with packing string from a plumbers' merchant or with PTFE tape pulled into a thin string. Pack it in with a screwdriver, then replace the gland nut and reassemble the tap.

Renewing the O-ring on a shrouded-head tap

1 Cut off the water supply to the tap and remove the tap handle and headgear in the same way as for renewing a washer.

2 Hold the headgear between your fingers and turn the spindle clockwise to unscrew and remove the washer unit.

3 Prise out the O-ring at the top of the washer unit with a screwdriver or penknife.

4 Smear the new O-ring with silicone grease, fit it in position, and reassemble the tap.

RELEASING THE SPINDLE

A non-rising spindle tap may have a circlip keeping the spindle in place. When you have removed the headgear, lever out the circlip so that you can gain access to the worn O-rings.

Renewing O-rings on a kitchen mixer tap

1 With both taps turned off, remove any retaining screw found behind the spout. If there is no screw, turn the spout to line up with the tap body and pull upwards sharply.

2 Note the position of the O-rings (probably two) and remove them.

3 Coat new O-rings of the correct size with silicone grease and fit them in position.

4 Smear the inside of the spout end with petroleum jelly, then refit it to the tap body.

Replacing shower-diverter O-rings

Diverters vary in design, but most have a sprung rod and plate attached to the diverter knob. When the knob is lifted, the plate opens the shower outlet and seals the tap outlet for as long as the shower is on.

1 With the bath taps turned off, lift the shower-diverter knob and undo the headgear nut with a spanner (probably 12mm size or use an adjustable spanner).

2 Lift out the diverter body and note the position of the washers and O-rings.

3 Remove the knob from the diverter body by turning it anticlockwise. You may need to grip it with a wrench.

4 Withdraw the rod and plate from the diverter body and remove the small O-ring at the top of the rod.

5 Grease a new O-ring of the correct size with silicone grease and fit it in place.

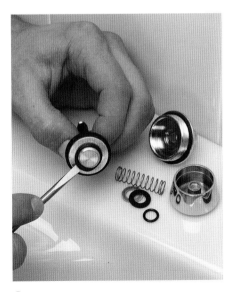

6 Replace all other rubber washers and O-rings on the base of the rod and plate. Old ones may have to be prised out.

Replacing a WC seat

Seats get broken over time, or the brackets may crack – or you may just want to replace an old seat with a new one to brighten up the bathroom. Whatever the reason, replacing a seat is a straightforward job.

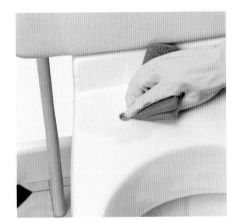

1 Undo the plastic wing-nuts under the rear of the toilet bowl and remove the old seat. Clean around the bolt holes and place the new seat in position.

2 Fit the supplied washers both above and below the bowl, two on each bolt. Finger-tighten the wing-nuts, check the seat is centred and tighten the nuts fully.

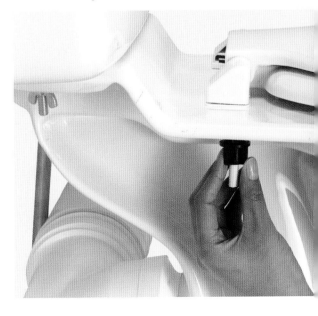

Energy efficiency

How efficient is your home?

A house that uses energy inefficiently, by allowing heat to escape through a poorly insulated loft, for example, will be expensive to run. As part of the new Home Information Packs, all houses for sale are assessed and given an energy rating. This chapter shows you what you can do to give your house the best possible rating.

Over time, heating and lighting an inefficient property will cost considerably more than running a home that is well insulated and fitted with energy-saving devices. So when you are buying a new home is it worth comparing the energy ratings of the properties you are considering and, if necessary, assessing the cost of improving them. The Home Information Pack will rate a property on a 120-point scale, divided into seven categories from A (most efficient) to G (least efficient) – this is the same A–G scale as is used to rate electrical appliances, such as washing machines and fridges.

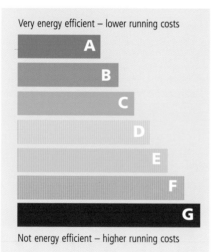

Very energy efficient – lower running costs

A

B

C

D

E

F

G

Not energy efficient – higher running costs

Where appropriate, the Home Information Pack will recommend measures that can be taken to increase the property's efficiency. These are graded by cost of installation and potential cost savings over a period of ten years.

Even if you are not buying or selling a house, there are many simple things you can do that can reduce your energy bills. These and the following pages will give you some pointers to assessing your own home. Your gas or electricity provider may also have an online survey you could take that will give you an energy rating and suggest low cost, higher cost and more significant upgrades and improvements you could consider.

Assessing your home

The age and construction of your home are the first things to consider: a new home with cavity walls, floor insulation and other energy-saving measures constructed to the latest Building Regulations requirements will, of course, be more energy-efficient than a Victorian property with draughty wooden floorboards and solid brick walls. You cannot change the fabric of your home, but work with what you have to make improvements where you can.

Walls
If you have cavity walls, make sure that they are insulated. Cavity wall insulation can save up to £160 a year on heating costs – and you may be eligible for a grant towards the installation costs. Solid walls are harder and more expensive to insulate, but they can be covered, either inside or outside, with a layer of insulating material. In practice, this is most feasible if you are undertaking a major renovation project and can insulate the walls on the inside as you gut and refit each individual room. Bear in mind that the rooms will be made slightly smaller by the thickness of the insulation on each external wall.

Roof and loft
All lofts should be well insulated, although it is also important to allow a little ventilation into the roof space to prevent damp forming. If your loft is not currently insulated, installing a 270mm thickness of insulation (the standard required by Building Regulations in new builds) across the whole area could cut your bills by up to a third. Topping up existing insulation to at least 250mm deep will also help and some grants are available to help with the work. Your own energy provider may also have a scheme to encourage customers to fit adequate loft insulation.

Windows and doors
Single-glazed windows are the least efficient insulators, and old windows with decaying wooden frames that may be draughty should be replaced. Make sure

that all windows and doors are fitted with appropriate draught excluders (pages 116–17) and that the frames are in good condition (page 19). Where possible, fit double-glazed units with the largest possible gap between panes to maximise the insulation efficiency (page 113). All new windows must comply with Part L (conservation of fuel and power) of the Building Regulations – ask your window supplier for advice.

Hot water
Make sure that your hot water cylinder and hot water pipes are lagged to minimise heat loss. Most modern hot water cylinders have a hard coat of sprayed-on lagging. If you have a bare metal cylinder, wrap it in a lagging jacket immediately. They can cost as little as £10 but will reduce heat loss by 75%, making your water heating instantly more efficient. Lag any accessible pipes around the cylinder and in the loft. Solar panels can also be installed and are an efficient system for heating water.

Central heating
The central heating system is one of the main energy users in the home. The most efficient type of boiler is a condensing boiler. These are expensive to fit, but over their lifetime you will more than recoup that cost in savings, particularly if you are planning to remain in a house for some years. If your boiler needs replacing always try to choose a condensing type.

REGULATIONS
Replacing a boiler, installing new windows and inserting cavity wall insulation are all categories of work that are subject to Building Regulations control. If you are uncertain whether you need approval for work you are planning, call your local council's Building Control Officer for advice.

An efficient combination of programmer and thermostat is also important to avoid using the boiler and heating rooms when it is not necessary. Consider how you use your house, whether you are at work during the day, and whether there are elderly people or young children in the family, who may need the temperature to be a little warmer.

Many programmers allow you to set a different heating schedule for weekdays and weekends. The most efficient types allow you to specify different temperatures at different times of day, see page 124.

For maximum efficiency, combine a single main room thermostat with individual thermostatic radiator valves (TRVs) throughout the house. This way, each room can be controlled separately, avoiding heating spare bedrooms or other little-used rooms to the same level as main bedrooms and living spaces.

Lights
Energy-saving light bulbs last between 6 and 15 times longer than standard bulbs and replacing a standard 100W light bulb with a 20W low energy light bulb can save around £12 per year in electricity costs. They are available in a wide range of styles and wattages to suit all kinds of lamps and fittings. Replacing all the bulbs in a house at once can be a costly exercise, but buy a selection of low-energy bulbs and fit them in place of standard bulbs each time an existing bulb blows.

Appliances
If you are fitting integrated appliances in a kitchen or buying a house with them already installed, always ask whether they are Energy Saving Recommended. Where possible, look for the most energy-efficient appliances, with an A, A+ or A++ rating.

Insulation and ventilation

Insulation is vital when making your home energy efficient. Building Regulations stipulate the level of insulation required in various parts of the house. Ventilation is also needed for the healthy circulation of air.

Roof insulation

A modern house with a pitched roof and a loft used for storage should have insulation between (and possibly over) the ceiling joists, about 200mm thick. On new builds, Building Regulations require 250mm. If the loft has been converted for use as a habitable room, the underside of the roof slope and the walls forming the loft room should be insulated to a similar standard. Flat roofs will incorporate insulation, probably as a warm roof structure.

If you have a pitched roof with less insulation than the current standards require, you can lay extra insulation over what is there already, or insulate the roof slope (see page 118). If you have a flat roof with inadequate insulation, consider converting it to a warm roof structure by adding insulation (see page 41).

Wall insulation

Modern homes incorporate insulation within their cavity walls to meet Building Regulations requirements. Timber-framed houses have insulation within their load-bearing wall panels. Older houses with unfilled cavity walls can be insulated by pumping insulation material into the cavity through holes drilled in the outer leaf of the wall. This is a job that must be carried out by an approved installer, and requires Building Regulations approval to ensure that the walls are in suitable condition, and that the installation fills the cavity entirely.

Houses with solid walls have poor insulation performance, and improving this is a major undertaking. It can be done by insulating and dry-lining the external wall surfaces indoors using a series of battens and plasterboard.

External insulation is a less disruptive but more expensive option, which may need planning consent. It involves fixing insulation material to the wall surfaces and waterproofing it with timber or tile cladding, or with a layer of rendering applied over expanded metal mesh. It is a job for a specialist contractor.

Floor insulation

Houses with solid ground floors built since the early 1990s have to include a layer of insulation to meet Building Regulations requirements. Older houses have no such insulation, so ground floor slabs can feel very cold. Adding insulation involves laying rigid polystyrene boards over the existing floor surface and adding a new floating floor of chipboard – a process that raises the existing floor level by at least 70mm.

Suspended timber ground floors are easier to insulate, because insulation can be placed between the floor joists. However, the job will involve lifting and re-laying floorboards unless there is an accessible crawl space below the floor. Adding 100mm thick rigid insulation will improve the floor's insulation significantly.

Window and door insulation

Recently built and modernised houses will benefit from double-glazed windows, and efficiently draughtproofed door and window frames. In older houses, replacing existing single-glazed windows with double-glazed ones will significantly improve their insulation performance (see page 114). Replacing the glass in existing windows with double-glazed sealed units may be possible depending on the design of the frames, but may be as expensive as replacing the windows. Installing secondary glazing inside the existing windows will be cheaper but is not as effective.

If existing doors and windows are not draughtproofed, installing the relevant products is a simple job to tackle on a DIY basis (see pages 115–17).

Ventilation

Appropriate ventilation is essential in four main areas of the home.
• Lofts must be ventilated to prevent condensation within the roof space.
• Voids beneath suspended timber ground floors need ventilation to prevent rot.
• Kitchens and bathrooms need ventilation to disperse cooking odours and steam. Extractor fans are useful for this.
• Adequate ventilation is mandatory in rooms containing fuel-burning appliances such as boilers and gas fires.

Choosing double glazing

Double glazing – having two layers of glass instead of one in a window – traps a layer of still air or inert gas between the panes. This acts as an insulator, but the warm inner pane also reduces cold down-draughts from the window and prevents condensation. Although double glazing will not save much on fuel bills, it will greatly increase indoor comfort. There are two main types – single sealed units and secondary double glazing.

Sealed units Two panes of glass separated by a spacer are bonded together and sealed at the factory before being fitted into the window frame. The panes may be separated by between 6 and 24mm; wide gaps give better insulation than narrow ones.

Secondary double glazing A pane of glass or plastic is fixed to the window frame, leaving an air gap between it and the existing glass. This is less effective than a sealed unit unless the opening part of the window is well draught-proofed. Condensation in the gap can be a problem in cold weather.

Triple glazing A wide air gap between panes of glass (100–200mm) insulates effectively against noise, but is too wide to retain heat. Triple glazing combines a sealed twin-pane unit with a third pane, like secondary glazing, to provide excellent heat and sound insulation.

Replacement windows

Many householders acquire double glazing when having old windows replaced. All double glazing companies offer windows (usually made from uPVC – unplasticised polyvinyl chloride – with steel internal reinforcement) that are fitted with tailor-made sealed units.

Since April 2002, all window and door installations have had to be carried out by a FENSA (Fenestration Self-Assessment) registered company. The contractor should give you a certificate to show that the double glazing units comply with the latest Building Regulations. In particular the regulations state that any uPVC windows must have a Thermal Insulation U-value of $2.0W/(m^2.K)$ and aluminium windows $2.2W/(m^2.K)$.

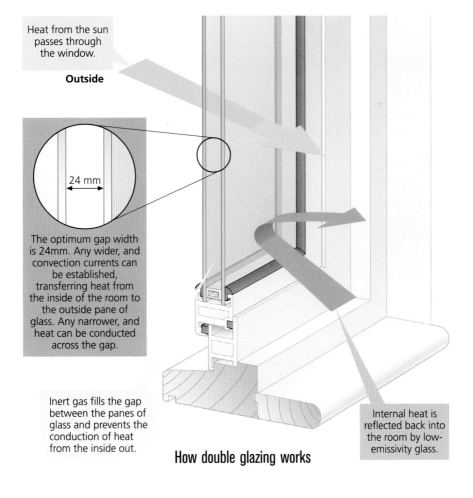

Heat from the sun passes through the window.

Outside

24 mm

The optimum gap width is 24mm. Any wider, and convection currents can be established, transferring heat from the inside of the room to the outside pane of glass. Any narrower, and heat can be conducted across the gap.

Inert gas fills the gap between the panes of glass and prevents the conduction of heat from the inside out.

Internal heat is reflected back into the room by low-emissivity glass.

How double glazing works

Replacing double-glazed panes

Cracked or failed double-glazed units that are letting in condensation should be replaced promptly to maintain their efficiency. The method depends on the type of unit.

Before you start Double glazing units must be bought ready-made to the size of your window from a glass merchant or double glazing supplier.

Sealed stepped units

Replacing sealed stepped double glazing is similar to fitting a single sheet of glass, except that spacer blocks are fitted in the rebate of the window to keep the stepped part of the double-glazed unit clear of the frame.

Retain the old spacer blocks so they can be re-used, or buy new ones from your glass merchant. Window companies are unlikely to sell them.

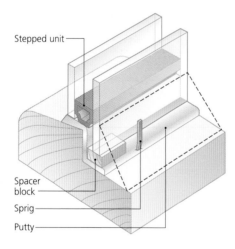

Stepped unit
Spacer block
Sprig
Putty

1 Place the spacer blocks in a bed of putty about 300mm apart along the bottom of the rebate.

2 Stand the double-glazed pane on the blocks and fix it in place with sprigs all round. Apply putty to the outside of the window in the normal way.

Square-edge units

Glazing beads are usually screwed into the outside of the window to hold square-edged double glazing units in place.

1 Unscrew the glazing beads before removing the broken glass.

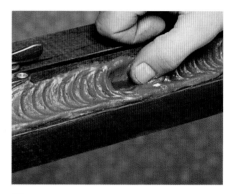

2 Put a bed of non-setting putty (available from glass merchants) around the rebate. Press spacer blocks into the putty (two blocks spaced well apart on each of the four sides).

3 Lift the sealed unit into place on the spacers and press it well back into the rebate.

4 Coat the glazing beads with non-setting putty on the inside face and press them tightly in place against the glazing units.

5 Fix the beads in place with brass screws.

Aluminium or plastic windows

The glass is often in rubber gaskets, making replacement difficult. Call in a glazier, or ask the manufacturer for details on glass replacement for your particular model of window.

Draughtproofing a window

Draughtproofing your windows is a simple and effective way of reducing heatloss and therefore improving the energy efficiency of your home.

Before you start Clean the window frame with water and a little washing-up liquid to remove all grease and dirt. Rinse and wait for the surface to dry.

A casement window

Most of the draughtproofing strips on the market (see page 117) are suitable for use on a wooden casement window. Only the strips with an adhesive backing can be used on a metal casement window.

1 Cut lengths to fit with scissors or a trimming knife.

2 Peel away the protective backing as you stick down each length on the rebate. Make sure that one piece of excluder goes right into each corner.

Silicone sealant for large gaps For large or uneven gaps, a silicone sealant (also called a frame sealant) is particularly useful, but cannot be used on sash windows. It can also be used on doors. Read any advice on the container before you begin.

A sash window

Rigid brush strip is the most suitable material for sealing the sides of a sash window, as the sashes slide over it easily.

1 Measure the height of the sliding sashes and cut four pieces of brush strip – two pieces for each sash.

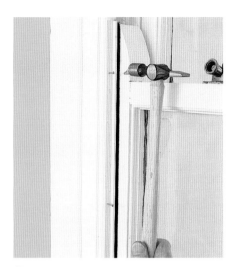

2 Fix the strip to either side of the frame: on the inside of the inner sash and on the outside of the outer sash. Use pre-holed strip, fixing it with the pins provided and a hammer. Unless the window is not opened very often, self-adhesive strip is not suitable because it is unlikely to withstand the friction from the sashes as they slide. Replace the sashes and beading.

3 Seal the gap at the top and bottom of the sashes with any of the more durable foam strips fixed to the frame or the sash.

4 If there is a draught between the top and bottom sashes of the window, fix nylon brush pile strip to the bottom sash at the meeting point.

Draughtproofing a door

You may need to use more than one type of draught excluder on a door. Fix a foam strip around the sides and top of a door and a threshold excluder at the bottom for a snug finish.

If you are fitting one of the foam, rubber or flexible strips for the first time – or are unsure which excluder is most suitable – experiment on one door before you buy all the material you need. To calculate how much of a strip draught excluder you need to buy, measure the height and width of the door.

Some threshold excluders are designed to deflect in-blown rain as well as to stop draughts. Threshold excluders are usually sold in standard lengths for external doors and some come in two parts: one to fix to the base of the door while the other part is fixed to the sill.

Adding an enclosed porch

If you put an enclosed porch around an outside door – especially if it is exposed to prevailing winds – you will greatly reduce the draughts entering the house. You will also help to reduce condensation inside if you can leave wet umbrellas and coats in a porch.

There are regulations that govern extending in front of the house building line, but porches are exempt from needing planning permission, providing the floor area is not more than 3m², and no part is higher than 3m above ground level. You must also ensure that the porch is at least 2m from the boundary between the garden and a road or public footpath. Porches are also exempt from Building Regulations control if the floor area is less than 30m².

HELPFUL TIP

If you cannot find the source of a draught, light a candle and hold it in front of the door or window. Move around the edge of the frame and the flame will flicker at the point where the draught is coming in. Take care not to set curtains alight.

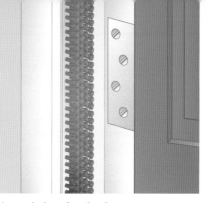

Strip excluders for the frame
Self-adhesive foam strips or nylon brush strip are cut to length and fitted to the frame. Some require pinning.

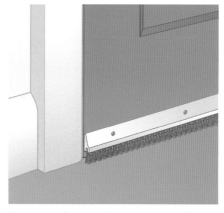

Strip excluders for the base of the door
A strip of nylon, rubber or plastic bristle mounted in aluminium. The excluder is fitted to the base of the door – on the inside – and is usually adjustable for height to give a good seal.

Letterbox excluder A plastic frame with two rows of nylon bristle fits over the inside of a letterbox.

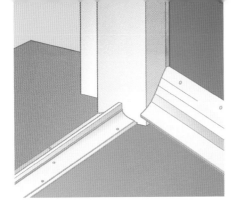

Two-piece excluders fitted to door and sill
A weatherbar is attached to the sill and a deflector is attached to the base of the door. The deflector is shaped to deflect rainwater over the weatherbar when the door is closed and the weatherbar prevents rain from being blown in beneath the door.

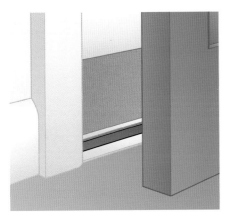

Metal or rubber seal for the sill
A plastic or metal bar fitted to the sill has a rubber insert which seals the gap under the door when it is closed.

Keyhole cover A pivoted cover, or escutcheon, hangs in front of the keyhole of a mortise lock.

Choosing a draught excluder

Before you buy a draught excluder, measure the width of the gaps that need to be blocked. The packaging on most draught excluders indicates how big a gap the product is intended to fill and where it can be used.

Self-adhesive foam strip Use on casement windows and exterior doors. Quality varies a lot. Some strips perish after only one or two seasons; more expensive types will last for five years or more. Cheaper versions are made of polyurethane, which hardens with age. Sizes vary according to the manufacturer but strips are usually about 6mm thick and 10mm wide. Most strips are only supplied in white. Avoid getting paint on foam – it will harden with age, unless the strip manufacturer states otherwise.

Self-adhesive rubber strip Use on casement windows and exterior doors. Available in a limited colour range and in profiles including P and E. This type of excluder is tough and will last longer than foam. Fix to the frame as for self-adhesive foam strip (above).

Brush strips Use on exterior and patio doors, and on sash and casement windows. The strips consist of siliconised nylon pile in self-adhesive strips or in a metal plastic holder that is to be tacked to the frame, not the door or window. The strip is particularly designed for surfaces which move against each other, as on sash windows and patio doors.

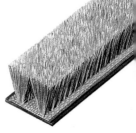

Insulating a loft

If the loft space is used only for storage then insulate the floor. But if the loft has been turned into a room – or if you plan to convert it into a room – insulate the roof slope.

If you put down flooring-grade chipboard after you have insulated between the joists, you will have a useful storage area. But remember the joists are only ceiling joists for the room below, not floor joists, so you cannot use the space as a room or store too many heavy things there.

Before you start Clear the floor space as much as possible and vacuum-clean the loft. At the same time, check for woodworm and rot, and, if necessary, call in a specialist contractor to treat it.
　　If the loft has no lighting, connect an inspection lamp to a socket downstairs or run a table lamp off an extension cable. A torch will not give adequate light for the job.

Fixing a vapour barrier on the floor

Tools *Scissors.*

Materials *Rolls of reflective foil building paper or sheets of polythene; masking tape.*

1 Cut the material with scissors so that it is about 50–75mm wider than the gap between the joists.

2 Lay the material in the gap. Remember that reflective foil paper must be laid foil-side down.

3 Seal any overlaps in the material with 50mm masking tape.

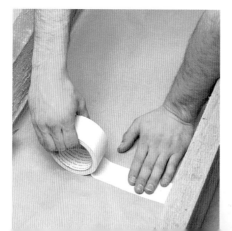

Laying insulation blanket on the floor

The spacing between joists varies but about 350mm is average. Do not cut the excess off a 400mm blanket – let it curl up on each side to make a snug fit.

Tools *Scissors; face mask; protective gloves.*

Materials *Rolls of glass fibre or mineral wool blanket.*

1 Start unrolling the blanket between two joists at the eaves at one end of the loft.

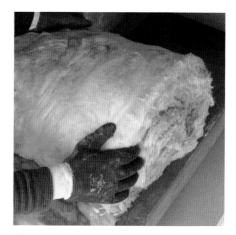

2 Do not take the material right into the eaves; you must leave a gap of about 50mm so that air can come in through the soffit and flow through the loft. If the air cannot circulate, condensation may form.

3 Press the blanket down lightly as you unroll it so that it lies flat but do not squash it so that it becomes compressed.

PROTECTING YOURSELF

Insulating products can be very irritating. Open the packaging in the loft and keep the hatch closed while you are working. Wear protective gloves and overalls or a long-sleeved shirt, and tuck sleeves and trouser legs into gloves and socks. If fibres do get into the gloves, they will cause more irritation than if you wore no gloves at all. Wear a face mask and throw it away after use. Wear a safety helmet to protect your head against the rafters.

4 When you reach the other side of the loft, cut the blanket with scissors, again taking care not to block where essential ventilation comes in under the eaves.

5 Continue to lay insulation between the other joists.

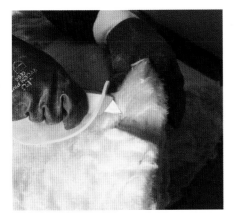

6 When joining two rolls, make a butt join, pressing the ends close to each other. Cut the insulation so that it fits tightly around pipes.

7 Try to slip insulation under loose electric cables to prevent them overheating. Where practicable, fix cables to the sides of the joists to keep them out of the way.

8 Never insulate under the cold water cistern. Leave a gap in the insulation so that warm air from below will keep the chill off the base of the cistern and help to prevent the water from freezing.

HELPFUL TIP

When laying insulation blanket, use a broom to push the blanket into the areas that are hard to reach.

Insulating with loose-fill

Pour loose-fill granules between the joists and level out. Make a levelling gauge so that the granules are at an even depth. Most ceiling joists are 100–150mm deep so filling level with the top will not provide adequate insulation. The top of the joists must be raised by nailing 50mm square battens to them. Do not spread insulation on top of the joists as you cannot see where it is safe to walk.

Cut a piece of scrap wood to a wide T-shape that will fit the gap above the loose-fill. The 'arms' should rest on top of the joists, so that when you run the gauge between two joists the granules are spread to a consistent depth.

THE IMPORTANCE OF VENTILATION

A good flow of air across the loft is important for keeping the roof timbers dry. In old lofts without roofing felt under the tiles or slates, air blows in and out through the gaps. If the roof has a layer of felt under the battens, then this prevents air coming in. Some modern roofs have ventilation around the eaves and also often at high level. Any insulation laid under the felt on the underside of the roof slope must allow ventilation to continue in order to clear any moisture from the surface of the felt. A gap of 50mm behind the insulation is usually enough to ensure good ventilation, provided there is room at the ridge for the air to escape and room at the eaves for it to enter.

LAGGING A LOFT-HATCH DOOR

• Cut a piece of glass-fibre or mineral-fibre blanket or thick expanded polystyrene sheet to fit above the loft hatch.
• To fix the blanket, hammer two or three nails along each edge of the door. Tie string over the material and loop it around the nails to hold it in place. Do not pull the string so tight that it squashes the blanket.
• Alternatively, cut a piece of polythene sheet large enough to cover the blanket. Fix the sheet over the blanket, holding the edges in place with drawing pins.
• If you are using polystyrene sheet, stick it to the door with polystyrene ceiling tile adhesive.
• Make sure that the hatch door is a tight fit. Fix a draught excluder (see page 117) to the rebate so that damp air cannot pass through into the cold loft above and possibly cause condensation problems.

Choosing loft insulation

You can insulate a loft yourself with blanket, loose fill or sheet insulation or pay a specialist company to blow loose-fill insulation between the joists. If you do it, lay at least 250mm of insulation: the minimum recommended in the current Building Regulations. A thicker layer will prevent even more heat loss. You may be eligible for a grant – ask your local council or Citizens Advice Bureau for details.

Before you buy Find out if a supplier will deliver the insulation. Blanket rolls and sacks of loose-fill are very bulky for their weight. Most cars will only hold a fraction of the amount needed for most lofts.

How much material do I need?
Calculate the size of your loft before buying the insulation material. Measure the overall length and width of your house and multiply the two figures. Most suppliers will advise on how much material is needed for a given area.

Blanket rolls Mineral wool or glass-fibre blanket is supplied in rolls 100–200mm thick. Standard rolls are 400mm wide; combi-rolls are 1200mm wide and have guidelines so the roll can be cut accurately into two 600mm wide or three 400mm wide pieces.
• Use a panel saw to cut through the roll while it is still in its wrapper, or you can cut through single widths with sharp scissors.
• Fibre blanket is cheap and effective, but tends to compress as it ages.
• Insulation is not effective if water condenses in the material. Choose blanket sleeved in polythene which acts as a vapour barrier. If you are using unbacked blanket, lay a vapour barrier before you insulate.

Plain blanket

Sleeved blanket

Mineral fibre batts Multipurpose semi-rigid batts can be used instead of fibre blanket in any insulation job. They are available from 25mm to 100mm thick so two or more batts are needed to meet the minimum depth required for insulating a floor. Batts are 1200mm long and 600mm or 900mm wide, which makes them much less bulky and easier to handle than blanket rolls – but they are more costly.

Loose fill This is supplied in sacks each sufficient to insulate 1m² and simply poured between the joists. The depth of the joist may need to be increased so that the required depth of cover is achieved.

• Common loose-fill materials are vermiculite granules, mineral fibre or polystyrene. Granules can also be used to top up old blanket insulation.
• Granules will blow about in a draughty loft, so pin building paper to the joists over the granules. Leave the tops of the joists visible so you can walk safely.
• Allow for joists when estimating quantities – or there will be too much left over.

Expanded polystyrene sheets Useful for sliding into areas which have been boarded over or which are difficult to reach – the flat roof over an extension, for example. It can also be used to insulate a cold water cistern, but is too expensive for a whole loft.
• Expanded polystyrene is available as squeeze-fit 60mm thick slabs 610 x 402mm and as 50mm thick general purpose 1200 x 450mm sheets. Specialist outlets will also cut polystyrene to exact requirements. Make sure it is fire retardant. Type A FRA will conform to BS4735 for combustibility.

Reflective foil building paper Acts as a vapour barrier so that moisture cannot condense in the insulation material. Heat also reflects off the shiny surface – either back into the house in winter or back into the loft in summer.
• Lay the foil between joists or drape it over them. If using it between joists to stop loose granules blowing about, pin the paper in position. There is no need to pin it if it is laid on the floor beneath insulation material.
• Supplied in 25m or 50m rolls 900mm wide by builders' merchants.

Insulating a roof

If you want to use your loft for storing items that need to be kept warm and dry it is advisable to insulate the underside of the roof. This will also keep the loft cooler in summer.

Tools *Knife or large pair of scissors; staple gun. Possibly power drill.*

Materials *Glass-fibre insulation batts; garden netting. Building paper, hardboard sheets or foil-faced plasterboard; drywall screws.*

1 Hold a length of insulation up to the underside of the roof and mark the width of the rafter gaps on the insulation.

2 Using scissors or knife, cut the insulation to fit between the rafters. Small off-cuts can be placed in the eaves first, to provide a spacing to maintain the air gap.

3 Do not hammer anything into the rafter because you could dislodge a tile or slate. Use a staple gun and nylon garden netting to hold the insulation in place. You may need a helper with this part of the task.

4 For a quick, simple finish, staple sheets of building paper to the rafters. Where two strips of building paper join, make sure they overlap by at least 100mm and tape along the join with waterproof adhesive tape. Alternatively, screw hardboard sheets to the rafters.

5 For an even better finish, you can screw foil-faced plasterboard to the rafters, as shown. The foil should face the roof. Use plasterboard drywall screws, which can be put in with a power drill.

Coping with a flat roof

Flat roofs should be insulated at the time they are built. If you are having an extension added to your house, make sure that insulation is incorporated when the roof is constructed.

Flat roofs must be ventilated above the insulation to prevent condensation on the timbers. You can do this by drilling small holes in the fascia or soffit board to take ventilator insect screens.

• If an existing roof lacks insulation, remove a fascia board so that you can see into the space between the roof lining and ceiling. The fascia board will either be nailed or screwed to the ends of the ceiling joists.

• Slide sheets of expanded polystyrene – 75mm thick – into the gap. If you cannot take off a fascia board, line the ceiling below, preferably with thermal board.

• You can place insulation above the roof decking if access to the roof void is not possible. The simplest method involves laying sheets of rigid polystyrene or other expanded foam insulation on the roof decking, covering it with a permeable geotextile membrane and placing a layer of ballast on top to keep it in place.

Insulating hot and cold water pipes

Water pipes should be lagged to reduce heat loss and to avoid winter freeze-ups.

Before you start Concentrate first on pipes that run across a loft, above an insulated floor, and those that run along outside walls in unheated rooms. Overflow and vent pipes that are exposed to the cold should also be lagged. Some pipes are boxed in. To lag them, unscrew the box and stuff pieces of glass fibre insulation all round the pipes. Make sure all pipes are clean and dry before you start.

Lagging pipes with self-adhesive foam wrap

Tools *Scissors.*

Materials *Rolls of self-adhesive foam wrap.*

Self-adhesive foam wrap is useful where there are many bends in the pipes and it would be difficult to use flexible foam tubes.

1 For pipes in the loft, begin work at the cistern. Cut pieces of foam wrap to a workable length with scissors.

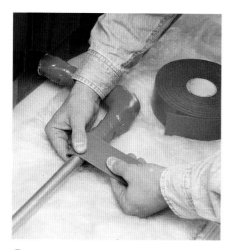

2 Wrap foam round the pipe, making generous overlaps of about one-third of the width of the wrap. Take care to cover the pipe well at bends – these are the vulnerable areas most likely to freeze.

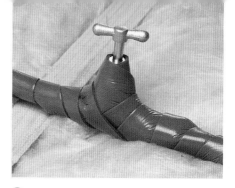

3 Take the wrap around any valves or stoptaps as you meet them, leaving only the handle exposed.

Lagging pipes with flexible foam tube

Tools *Scissors; serrated knife.*

Materials *Foam tube to match pipe size; adhesive tape; plastic clips.*

1 Lag the pipes leading from the cistern first, if you are insulating pipes in the loft. Wrap plastic adhesive tape around the first tube to hold it in place, even if the tube is one of the self-locking types. Push it up tight against the cistern so that the tank connector joint is covered.

2 Butt-join the tubes where they meet and wrap around the join to hold them tight. Cut the tube at 45° to fit it round elbows and tee fittings, and tape the joints. Alternatively secure joints with plastic clips.

3 Cut the tube to fit around the body of a gatevalve as closely as possible.

Choosing a boiler

The type of boiler you have can make a crucial difference to your home's energy efficiency and carbon dioxide rating. If a boiler is more than 15 years old the chances are that it is no longer working efficiently and should be replaced, though regular servicing will extend a boiler's useful life. A recent survey by the Energy Savings Trust found that as many as 64 per cent of home buyers would be put off buying a house with an ancient and inefficient boiler. So replacing your boiler may have financial benefits as well as environmental ones.

What type of boiler do you have?

Conventional boiler Conventional boilers heat water in a heat exchanger, rather like a gas-ring under an old-fashioned kettle. Most are designed for use on fully-pumped open-vented systems.

Combination boiler Also known as a 'combi' boiler, this is a central-heating boiler and multi-point water heater all in one. Hot water for the radiators is heated in its own circuit (usually sealed) in the normal way, but the boiler also heats cold water from the mains, delivering it on demand. The main advantages are the savings in space – no hot water cylinder or tanks make them a popular choice in flats – a constant supply of hot water and better water pressure in showers.

Back boiler A back boiler is a heat exchanger located behind a gas fire. It works in much the same way as a conventional boiler. Although many still exist in older houses, they are no longer an option for a new fitting for most people.

Condensing boiler Most new boilers are this type (see box, right).

Replacing an old boiler

By law most new gas boilers must now be high-efficiency condensing boilers (with a few exceptions depending on suitability). This also applies to oil-fired boilers from April 2007. Replacing an old boiler with a new condensing model can save up to a third on annual heating bills.

Energy ratings
• Energy rating labels allow you to compare boilers' efficiency and therefore running costs. Boilers are rated according to how much of the fuel they consume is converted into heat. The ratings range from A to G, with A being the most efficient.
• Look out for the Energy Saving Trust's recommended logo. Only A-rated boilers, with an efficiency of over 90 per cent, may carry this logo.

CONDENSING BOILERS

With a larger heat-exchanger than a conventional boiler, a condensing boiler is designed so that the water returning from the heating system is used to cool the flue gases from the water heater, extracting extra heat that is normally lost through the flue. They are meant to be used with a fan-assisted balanced flue and in a fully-pumped system. When the flue gases are cooled, water vapour will condense and so a pipe has to be installed to drain this water away. Condensing boilers convert more than 88 per cent of their fuel into heat, compared to 78 per cent for conventional types. Condensing boilers are available for use with gas, LPG or oil. Combination condensing boilers are available, too.

• You can compare the efficiency of your current boiler with other models at www.boilers.org.uk

What size?
• It is crucial that a boiler is an appropriate capacity for the property it is serving. Consider whether you need your boiler to supply heating and hot water, how many people live in your household and how many bathrooms you need to service.
• Consider the space available – not just for the boiler, but also for a hot water cylinder and cold water tanks, and what the demands on the system are likely to be.

Installation and servicing
• A new or replacement boiler must always be installed by a CORGI or OFTEC engineer.
• Programmers and thermostats must be installed, too.
• Boilers must be serviced regularly and any faults dealt with by an expert.

Controlling your central heating

Efficient temperature and time controls can cut heating costs by up to 17 per cent.

Room thermostat This temperature-sensitive switch is set to a pre-selected room temperature. It sends an electrical signal to switch the heating on when the air temperature falls below the pre-set level, and off when it rises above the level.

A room thermostat is best placed in a draught-free spot on an inside wall away from direct sunlight, about 1.5m above floor level, and away from any heat sources.

By turning down the room thermostat by just 1°C you can cut 10 per cent off your heating bills.

Thermostatic radiator valve These valves regulate the flow of water through the radiators to which they are fitted, opening and closing according to the temperature in the room. If the room is cold, a full flow is allowed through to the radiator. Then as the room warms up, the valve closes to reduce the hot water flow through the radiator.

TRVs save money and energy by allowing you to set different temperatures in different rooms. Rooms facing south and rooms with open fires, other heaters or hot appliances, such as an oven, benefit most from TRVs. Most systems are compatible with TRVs. Seek expert advice on which ones to buy.

Programmers Time controls range from simple switches to complex electronic programmers. The most useful can time space heating and domestic hot water separately, so water heating can be turned on and off at the same times of day all year round, while space heating times can vary with the season. Electronic types can give

you three control periods a day and different settings for every day of the week. Some even have a 'holiday' setting.

Combined programmable thermostats give even more energy-efficient heating control. The programmer can be set to maintain different specified room temperatures depending on the time of day. This allows you to raise the temperature in the early morning or at bedtime and drop it to a lower level during the day, when people are dressed and active in the house.

Water heating control An electric thermostat on the outside of the hot water cylinder will control the water temperature. It operates a motorised valve to restrict the flow of water through the heating coil inside the cylinder. This saves energy because it means that hot water for taps is not heated as high as that for radiators.

Boiler energy management Sophisticated devices make sure that the boiler works only when needed. A boiler energy manager will reduce wasteful short cycling on a boiler – that is, when 'hot water only' is selected on a conventional central heating programmer, the boiler will continually switch on and off to keep the water in the boiler at the selected temperature. It will do this even though the hot water cylinder is already full of hot water. This 'short cycling' can add as much as 30 per cent to fuel bills.

The device will also take account of outside temperatures, and will regulate the central heating system accordingly. For example it will override the setting and delay the start time of the central heating on warmer days.

A,B,C

D,E,F

V,W

Acknowledgments

All images in this book are copyright of the Reader's Digest Association Limited, with the exception of those in the following list.

The position of photographs and illustrations on each page is indicated by letters after the page number:
T = Top; **B** = Bottom; **L** = Left; **R** = Right; **C** = Centre

6 iStockphoto.com **78** GE Fabbri Limited **101** GE Fabbri Limited **111** iStockphoto.com/Gordon Ball **115** GE Fabbri Limited. **Front cover** Martin Bennett

The majority of images were previously published in Reader's Digest *DIY Manual*, with the exception of the following:
65, 66 TL & R Reader's Digest *First-Time Homeowner's DIY Manual*
107 TR & BR Reader's Digest *How Everything In The Home Works*

Additional copyright includes **19** © Reader's Digest/HL Studios, **20 TR** © Reader's Digest/HL Studios, **42** © Reader's Digest/David Giles, **46 T** © Reader's Digest/HL Studios.

Reader's Digest Home Survey Manual is based on material in *Reader's Digest DIY Manual*, published by The Reader's Digest Association Limited, London.

First Edition Copyright © 2007
The Reader's Digest Association Limited,
11 Westferry Circus, Canary Wharf,
London E14 4HE
www.readersdigest.co.uk

Editor Alison Candlin

Art Editor Julie Bennett

Assistant Editor Celia Coyne

Editorial Consultant Mike Lawrence

Proofreader Ron Pankhurst

Indexer Marie Lorimer

Reader's Digest General Books

Editorial Director Julian Browne

Art Director Nick Clark

Managing Editor Alastair Holmes

Head of Book Development Sarah Bloxham

Picture Resource Manager Sarah Stewart-Richardson

Pre-press Account Manager Sandra Fuller

Senior Production Controller Deborah Trott

Product Production Manager Claudette Bramble

Origination Colour Systems Limited, London
Printed and bound in China by CT Printing

The contents of this book are believed to be accurate at the time of printing. However the publisher accepts no responsibility or liability for any work carried out in the absence of professional advice.

We are committed to both the quality of our products and the service we provide to our customers. We value your comments, so please feel free to contact us on 08705 113366, or via our website at www.readersdigest.co.uk

If you have any comments about the content of our books, email us at gbeditorial@readersdigest.co.uk

ISBN: 978 0 276 44228 5
BOOK CODE: 400-613 UP0000-1
ORACLE CODE: 250010677H.00.24